Best u
he

LINDA ALEXANDER

It's Up

TO YOU

YOUR BLUEPRINT FOR A BETTER LIFE

First published by Need2Know 1998
This edition published by Need2Know 1998
Need2Know, 1-2 Wainman Road,
Woodston, Peterborough PE2 7BU

Edited by Anne Sandys
Typesetting by Forward Press Ltd

The people whose stories feature in this book are real; in some instances names have been changed to protect privacy.

IT'S UP TO YOU

Contents

What you can do or dream you can, begin it,
Boldness has genius, power and magic in it.
Johann Wolfgang von Goethe

To Sharon

and to everyone who chooses to claim their own
future.
Follow your dreams!

Author Acknowledgement

This book has been shaped by the hopes, experiences and insights of the hundreds of men and women with whom I have been privileged to work, on personal development courses and management training programmes throughout Britain. Special thanks to the named contributors who have shared their stories and to the following colleagues and friends whose help and support has been invaluable: Dr Allan Webster, Marion Morran, Jackie Leggat, Jill Brown, Jonathan Snell, John Brown, Linda Crouch, Janieann Wilson, Hilda Francis and the staff of the Women Onto Work project in Edinburgh.

I would also like to thank my husband Douglas, and children, Jamie, Lauren and Katherine. Episodes from our domestic life have provided a rich source of material, as readers will discover!

Foreword

Understanding that our opportunities and destinies - even our moods! - are in our own hands, is one of the most exciting and daunting discoveries one can make. It takes an incredible amount of self-knowledge and belief to rise to the challenge. *It's Up To You* is an invaluable book for anyone exploring the extent of their power for the first time, or who needs reminding.

Sue Tibballs, Campaigner
The Body Shop International

We all need strategies for survival and growth in an insecure world. So a practical guide to personal development which helps you create your own blueprint for success, is a good approach to follow. We're all more capable than we think!

Sarah Kennedy, Broadcaster and author
Presenter, BBC Radio 2 Morning Programme

Introduction

This book is written out of the belief that you and I have the power to choose or change the life we lead. In our rapidly-changing and uncertain world - in which potential and promise is often challenged or undermined - it is important that we have ways of empowering ourselves in order to create our own options and opportunities.

Personal development is a learning process. It is about recognising that you can make things happen for yourself and about realising that whilst you have one lifetime, you have limitless futures. You can grow your own!

This doesn't mean that we always have complete control over what happens to us, but that, whatever our personal situation, you and I have the power to create our own happiness and fulfilment. We need not be victims or martyrs, not hangers-on or heroes.

This is not stated lightly. There is no gain, as they say, without pain. And no solutions that don't ultimately begin with ourselves.

This is a *way of* book rather than a *how to* book. There are hundreds of *how to* books on the market which claim the formula for total success in life and love. And if, having read something along the lines of How To Get To The Top, How To Make A Million, How To Transform Your Life/Pet/Partner/Body/House/Child, you don't, haven't or can't, and you still feel over-stressed, over-weight and under-achieving, it's your own fault and you need to scour the shelves for books on how to raise your self-esteem!

It's not that these books don't contain any good ideas. They do. But to package a glib formula as the panacea for all life's problems is unreal. Life's not like that. And if where you're coming from is a never-ending cycle of *scraping by, making do,* or *putting up with despite,* then How To Get To The Top is probably less important that how to get to the end of the week.

This book, by contrast, offers you practical help to find your own way forward - to the end of the week and beyond - by taking the steps which have most meaning and relevance for you.

New horizons

It is designed as a way of opening up new horizons for individuals who feel they want to move on in some way from their current situation. It is a starter pack of sensible, realistic ideas to raise your awareness of your own options and choices and to help you exercise them.

The book therefore begins and ends with you, your feelings and experiences, your hopes and fears, the ways in which you view yourself and the ways in which you relate to the world around you. It offers you time to reflect and time to tune into yourself on a more personal level, so that you can begin to challenge assumptions and beliefs which limit you.

The ideas presented here have already been used to positive effect by men and women of different ages and stages of life, with different experiences, abilities, hopes and expectations. They may be particularly helpful to individuals whose home or work experiences have left them feeling unsettled, dissatisfied, vulnerable or fragile, ie in whom the urge and determination to move forward is already felt.

You can use the book in any or all of the following ways:

- as an overview of the subject
- to make changes in your life
- to plan skill or work development
- to challenge the limits you set yourself
- to support yourself when you're uncertain where to turn
- as an introduction to personal development tools and techniques
- to build trust and belief in your own abilities
- to set particular skills, such as assertiveness, within a wider context
- to value yourself
- to build confidence and self-esteem

Do it your way

The book is intended to help you do things *your* way. It is about what you can do to help yourself in whatever way suits you and your circumstances. You may, for instance, choose to make some changes in your life. While this is not always an easy process, it can be as rewarding as it is challenging, especially if you are in the driving seat.

So make the book work for you. You may find it beneficial to read through the chapters in order, because of the way they build on each other, but go with your natural instincts. A variety of approaches is used in presenting the content because everyone is different and your own knowledge and life experiences will breathe life into the material. You will also come up with lots of ideas of your own which may illustrate, contradict, reinforce or challenge the ideas presented here. That's great. Engage with the parts of the book which have the greater resonance for you and leave the rest.

The book fits together as follows:

Part 1 Know Yourself

is about ways of looking at yourself and the world around you. Developing knowledge about your current situation or starting point is the crucial first stage in your moving forward. It is both the place to begin and the place to return to, as you assess and re-assess your development and progress. Issues introduced in Part 1 will be developed later in the book, with specific references where appropriate. Don't worry if your thoughts seem disjointed at this stage. As you go through the book and consider your own experiences, your thoughts will begin to crystallise into a deeper awareness of your individuality and potential.

Part 2 Know Your Potential

is about ways of evaluating your strengths and using your personal power to turn plans into reality. You can have all the good intentions under the sun, but if you don't know how to turn them into achievable goals, they will never see the light of day. The goal-setting process described in Chapter 6 is deliberately placed in the middle of the book as a staging post, to help you organise your thoughts if you're reading from the beginning. But it can be used at any point and in any way that is appropriate to your personal action planning.

Part 3 Know The Challenges You Face

helps you identify ways of supporting yourself through
challenge and difficulty - living with change, fear and
stress without losing hope and direction. These are
elements which create the shades and shadows in our
life. The big issue is how we tackle them. So once
we've got this one sorted out, the sun will always
shine, the birds will always sing, the sky will always be
blue and your cellulite will have disappeared. So that's
all right then! Or not.

Part 4 Know The Skills You Need

explores way of developing the life skills needed to
realise your potential. This includes showing and
gaining respect in your relationships and caring for
your physical health and emotional well-being. It is
designed to consolidate your thinking about the ways
in which you can express yourself and relate to others
with increased comfort and confidence. The final
chapter closes on a nurturing note which focuses on
your capacity for rest, relaxation and renewal.

Each chapter ends with a summary and a set of action
points which are designed to help you turn theory into
practice. Some action points offer food for thought,
whilst others are pen and paper exercises to help you
identify particular steps or goals you may choose to
pursue. Many of the exercises can be adapted and used
for group working. Each chapter can also be dipped
into separately and used for reference, along with the
Help List at the back, so you can use the material to
suit your needs, whether you nibble the book in bite-
sized chunks or eat it whole.

Good Luck!

Part One

Know Yourself

Chapter 1

Your Starting Point

*The real voyage of discovery consists not in seeking new lands
but in seeing with new eyes.*
Marcel Proust

- Your roles
- Mind that attitude
- Look inside
- What drives you?
- Action Points
- Summing up . . .

We begin by exploring the nature of your individuality
and the ways in which you relate to the world around
you. You live, you breathe, you have 656 muscles, one
life and limitless futures. But who on earth are you?
It's good to tackle a big question!

But it's often easier and less scary to start with a
smaller one. Your responses to the smaller questions in
this book, as in life generally, will build a bigger
picture, which will help you decide the big question of
who you are. What do you see below?

The way you see these shapes will be your reality, seen through your eyes. You've probably already guessed though, that there's another view, another way of seeing the same thing. You might not see it until it's pointed out to you and even then, it may or may not be obvious. But it will still be real. One picture, two views. Both right, both real. Do you see a set of black shapes or the word FIT - or both?

- How do you picture yourself?
- How do other people see you?
- *Is there a difference?*

Exploring your own view of yourself and understanding how others perceive you, is a vital first step to getting to grips with your own future.

Your Roles

No man, said the poet John Donne, is an island. And most of us live our lives necessarily amidst the bustle and chaos of meeting other people's expectations as well as our own.

So it is necessary in exploring ourselves and our world, that we should take account of those closest to us, whose demands may bring us both fulfilment and conflict.

My friend Susie, for example, would make a great circus performer - she's a born juggler. She juggles her responsibilities as if her life depended on it. And her life does depend on it, because so many people depend on her - her mum, her young children, her sister, her elderly aunt, her boss, her partner, her sister-in-law *and* the dog. Keeping all the balls in the air can be very difficult, and even Susie drops a few now and then. 'What can I do?' she wails, as she collapses in a dishevelled heap at the end of *one of those days*. 'They need me.'

Role call

Many people gain their sense of identity from their roles or areas of their lives in which they accept a responsibility. Defining how we feel about them can help us gain an insight into the sort of person we are and the way we relate to those closest to us.

You may find it helpful to list your various roles. My own list would include: *mother, daughter, partner, professional trainer, sister, friend, colleague* and *voluntary worker*. Each of these roles involves things I actively enjoy doing, things I don't mind doing and things I probably rather resent, by which I don't just mean cleaning the toilet. Though even this can pose a magnetic attraction when the alternative is sitting down to write a book!

Common threads

Each role invokes feelings which cover a kaleidoscope of emotions depending on the situation. Whilst my mother role brings out feelings of caring, contentment and not a little anxiety, my voluntary worker role as a citizen's advocate touches far more on feelings of frustration and anger at systems and procedures that devalue individuals. Perhaps the common threads are feelings and expressions of care and concern.

Try and work out the amount of time you spend in each role over the period of a week. Does the proportion of time you spend in each role match the importance you attach to it?

You may find it helpful to refer to the Timeframes exercise in Action Points at the end of Chapter 2.

Give and take

You can take this a stage further by exploring the *type* of support you offer and receive. This could include affection, advice, understanding, guidance, listening, practical care, information and money. Do you give as good as you get? Do you strike a balance between meeting others' expectations of you and meeting your own needs?

Comparing your roles can also broaden your understanding of what makes you tick. Which are the roles you find most enjoyable and fulfilling? Which are the most challenging? Which bring out more negative thoughts and feelings? Are there common factors which indicate your own strengths and preferences or even perhaps your pet dislikes and prejudices? It is important to think through these questions and be honest with yourself here.

No one can be responsible for the entire well-being and happiness of another individual, and it is useful to realise that too many expectations can create pressure to make difficult choices - which often results in feelings of guilt.

Just in case you're tempted to take on that kind of responsibility, take a tip from a colleague who returned hyped-up from one of those training seminars of the American kind, chanting the phrase . . .

Mind That Attitude

You are a person with attitude - lots of attitudes. Whether we inherit them through nature or cultivate them through nurture, they inform everything we do. And since everything we do dictates how others view us and behave towards us, our attitudes have a lot to answer for.

We tend to take the way we view things - our attitudes, assumptions and beliefs - all for granted. They bring order to our world. And some of them are vital to the safety and well-being not only of ourselves, but of those who depend on us. We rightly assume, for example, that if a child steps too close to an open fire, he or she will get burned, so we reduce this hazard by using a fireguard. Other assumptions are not as helpful or as accurate. So exploring just what our attitudes and beliefs are is important in order to evaluate their usefulness and validity to our current lives.

Never trust a man who wears white socks

Here are a few examples of assumptions which can result in all kinds of conflict, misinformation and discrimination . . .

- *Younger employees make better workers.*
- *No one's really poor nowadays.*
- *_____ is women's work and _____ is men's work.*
- *Homeless people choose to be so.*
- *Youngsters these days are completely irresponsible.*
- *What do you expect? They come from Glasgow /Leeds / Manchester etc.*
- *Disabled people are different.*

It's quite natural that when dealing with unfamiliar people, our judgements are based on generalised beliefs. As we get to know people better, we may amend our point of view. But it can be difficult to unlearn or discount our first impressions, whether those impressions are created by personal contact or word of mouth. This is one of the reasons why gossip can be so destructive . . .

'I heard that our new supervisor had left her last job under a cloud,' recalls Martin, an administrative worker, 'and that she was mentally unstable. So you can imagine how keen we were to have her leading the team! In the event, the gossip turned out to be completely unfair. She had apparently accused her previous boss of sexual harassment. As a result, she was off work with stress for months and only decided against pursuing the sexual harassment case for the sake of her health. She is an excellent team leader but still feels she has to prove herself.'

Here's a few more holes we may fall into . . .

- We assume that other people share our motives, values and ways of behaving, even though some people are as different from us as inhabitants of the planet Zog. And they may perceive *us* to be the aliens!

- We may act more favourably towards people who come from the same town/school/profession/ background as us.

- We may see what we expect to see, rather than what is in front of our eyes, eg what are the words you read in the triangle?

Many people read the phrase as 'Picnic in the park,' but the word 'the' is actually repeated.

Seeing what we expect to see, rather than what is actually there, is a common mistake - and not just in relation to words on a page.

Look Inside

If all this should make us guard against making judgements about other people too quickly, what about the judgements we make about ourselves? What's your attitude to *you*? Are you your own best friend or your own harshest critic? Perhaps you fall somewhere in between?

In general, if your assumptions and judgements about yourself are negative, this can create difficulties in your dealings with others, which in turn lowers your self-esteem. This makes it even less likely that you will enjoy positive relationships at work or at home and it can become a vicious circle which is difficult to break.

Our attitude to ourselves and others is a common theme of the book, which is revisited in Chapter 4 Personally Yours, Chapter 5 Creating Choices,

Chapter 9 Developing Assertiveness and Chapter 10 Developing Communication.

You hear it all the time . . .

What are your favourite put-downs? And what do they imply about the assumptions and beliefs you hold, which may be impeding your growth and development?

- *I'm so fat / old / weak / stupid / vulnerable / neurotic / guilty / out-of-date / useless . . .*

- *I've never been any good at relationships / practical tasks / being a mother / being a father / academic subjects / computers / looking after myself / speaking out / life . . .*

- *I'm just (only) a housewife / secretary / receptionist / labourer / tradesman / unemployed . . .*

Any of these sound familiar? I often ask workshop participants to list their positive qualities - things like *caring, reliable, supportive, thoughtful, patient, sociable, adaptable* and so on. It's like drawing teeth. The faces go blank. Yet if I ask the same people to list their best friend's or partner's personal qualities, there's no problem. Perhaps there's a natural reticence to credit ourselves for fear of being perceived to be bragging. We give bouquets to others and brickbats to ourselves! But seeing yourself in a more positive light isn't about self-indulgence, it's about self-respect.

Ifs and buts

These negative judgements are near cousins of the *ifs* and *buts* which also undermine our confidence and personal effectiveness . . .

- *I could have done anything I wanted, IF it weren't for my wife / husband / partner / daughter / son / boss / parent / cat / dog / gerbil / time of the month / day of the week / colour of the sky.*

- *I would love to go back to college / change jobs / finish the relationship / move house / lose weight BUT it'll have to wait UNTIL the children are older / my boss retires / I win the lottery / I'm married / I'm divorced / I have the time / I have the money / I have the opportunity . . .* the twelfth of never and that's a long, long time!

To this I would offer:

- If not now, when?
- If not you, who?

What Drives You?

It's generally accepted that highly-motivated people put more into life and are more likely to achieve their goals. Drive and inspiration come in all guises and can derive from crisis and chaos as well as kinder circumstances.

Margaret Brown (61) is a peer counsellor for people with disabilities. She was 21 when she lost her sight. She takes up the story . . . 'I was devastated to say the least. My husband left and I found myself on my own with three small children to look after. I thought my world had come to an end. But I didn't have time to wallow in my distress. The children were depending on me. I was determined to care for them to the best of my ability. This I managed to do, in spite of the poverty and degradation which we had to endure.

' I was apprehensive about asking for help from Social Services in case they took my children away. So I had little social contact outside the house. It was 25 years before I finally met another blind person. It's difficult to express how isolated I felt, but you get to a point beyond tears. I and the children worked together to adjust to the situation and I am proud of the way I brought them up.'

In later life, Margaret was driven to achieve in other ways. 'I still needed to achieve a purpose in life as a blind person, so a few years ago, I enquired about training and was assessed at the RNIB centre in Fife. There, I learned all types of skills from engineering to computing. Thereafter I studied at the Royal Blind School and the local college, gaining a sheaf of qualifications and much more confidence in my own abilities. Attending a women returners' course gave me work experience at the age of 60 at a college Sensory Centre, where I currently work on a casual basis. My motivation now stems from a wish to help other people with disabilities.'

Back to basics

One of the most useful ways of looking at human motivation was put forward by the behavioural scientist Abraham Maslow, who said that although the factors which drive and inspire people will change according to their situation, they follow a pattern or *hierarchy* of needs.* We strive to meet our most basic *(lower order)* needs first - our need for food, shelter and security.

* *Motivation And Personality - Harper & Rowe, New York, 1954*

Once these needs have been met, we progress to other
(higher order) needs - the need to belong, the need for
achievement and power and ultimately, the need for
self-fulfilment. When any of our basic needs are
threatened, however, we will go back to survival mode.

Maslow's hierarchy of needs

Let's look at each of the needs in turn.

Our need to survive - This one's pretty obvious. If I were
stranded on a desert island, with only myself and a
few palm trees for company, it wouldn't be my choice
of 10 favourite discs that would occupy my thoughts -
it would be my need for food and water. Sex is
another of the biological needs that would come into
this category, though in this scenario, not one I would
personally get hung up on!

Our need to be safe - Once I have taken care of my
immediate physical needs, the next thing on my mind
will be my safety. I need a fire at night and somewhere
to sleep. And I will exert myself to achieve this level of
security and freedom from fear and anxiety. You could
argue that we spend most of our lives on these two
basic needs - survival and security - whether it's
putting food on the table, ensuring a roof over our

heads, saving money for a rainy day etc. We may of course confuse needs with *wants*, but nevertheless, scant attention is often paid to what Maslow termed the higher order needs of belonging, achieving and fulfilling our potential.

Our need to belong - Satisfying this need on my desert island is impossible because this is my need to belong to and feel part of a relationship or group. In common with most people, I am a sociable animal and this is why I would eventually try to leave my desert island, notwithstanding my favourite music!

Our need to achieve - This need is connected with empowering ourselves to get results. On my desert island, I might decide to build a bigger and better shelter (than the neighbours?) thereby maintaining my survival needs too. This motive implies a need for status and recognition and often relates to developing existing skills.

Our need for self-fulfilment - This is the need to develop potential, to become more than you already are. This need will be frustrated on my desert island. Many people meet this need by contributing to society in some way or pursuing some activity to an extraordinary degree, either through a career or in their personal lives. Our own capability can motivate us to higher and higher things if other needs are satisfied. We climb mountains because they are there.

Still climbing

Where are you just now in the hierarchy of needs? Are you putting all your energy into surviving each day or are you busy fulfilling yourself in your career? Perhaps your needs and motivations have altered according to the different times and circumstances of your life.

Consider too, the activities you do in the course of a week which give you the most pleasure and fulfilment and think about which needs they satisfy. Many people who are keen members of sports and social clubs, for instance, will be aware of the sense of belonging which their group participation gives them. Family life, paid or unpaid work and hobbies can also provide outlets for our need to belong, to achieve and to fulfil ourselves.

Personal development is generally about these higher order needs, since they create the greatest challenges and opportunities for living a fuller life.

'When we talk about needs, we mean something more than human survival,' says the author Michael Ignatieff in *The Needs Of Strangers* (Hogarth Press 1990). 'We also use the word to describe what a person needs in order to live their full potential. What we need to survive and what we need to flourish are two different things. The aged poor in my street get just enough to survive. The question is whether they get what they need in order to live a human life.'

This is the moral imperative that underlines the growth of the advocacy movement, which aims to empower disadvantaged people to assert their right to live their lives as valued, responsible members of society.

Our needs and wants are crucial to how we define ourselves and we naturally fear their loss. This idea is discussed further in Chapter 5 Creating Choices and Chapter 8 Meeting Stress.

Action Points

- **Draw boundaries** - If you have a tendency to dance to other people's tunes, be aware that you *can* draw boundaries which help you act according to your priorities and your willingness / ability to give time, energy and commitment. If your elderly mother expects a twice-weekly visit, your partner expects a cooked evening meal, your children expect laundering and taxi services, your boss expects you to work overtime, and your friend expects you to babysit regularly, these demands can dominate your life. Make a note of others' expectations of you, if you like, as a first step to identifying the ones you'd like to negotiate or change.

- **Who are you?** - Jot down words and phrases (at least 10) which you feel sum up your personal qualities and characteristics. Eg *intelligent, sensitive, shy, loyal, quick-tempered, abrupt, anxious, impatient, a dry sense of humour, reserved nature.* This can be a difficult exercise, especially if you're not used to thinking of yourself in these terms.

  When you've drawn up your list, ask two or more people who know you well to do the same exercise *about* you.Then compare the results and discuss them, noting the similarities and differences. It may give you a new view of yourself! You can use this idea to compare perceptions of your strengths and weaknesses, as explained further in Chapter 5.

- **Bridge the gap** - Assess the image you currently present to the world, both in terms of the way you look and the way you behave. What image of yourself would you *ideally* present to the world? What issues does this raise for you?

- **Picture yourself** - Create a picture of your own development over the years by asking yourself the following questions about changes in your life, using whatever timeframes are appropriate, perhaps 20 years ago, 10 years ago and 5 years ago.

  - How did being male / female affect my life?
  - How did I spend my time?
  - What sort of clothes did I wear?
  - What food did I enjoy?
  - Who were the most important people in my life?
  - What did I enjoy doing most?
  - What were my ambitions?
  - What were the main advantages and disadvantages of being my age then?

- **Building up or pulling down?** - Don't put yourself down. Some people undermine their achievements so much that they almost disappear. Have an agreement among your close friends that you don't do it *to* each other, *about* each other or *in front of* each other! You can spot the phrases . . . *I've never been able to do _____; I'll have a go, but I'm sure I'll make a mess of it; I wish I was like _____, they are so much brighter / more able / experienced; Yes, I was successful, but I was very lucky* etc etc.

- This also applies if you have the habit of constantly apologising. You, of course, are *not* the sort of person who will apologise for someone else's mistake, for the state of the house (ie not quite spotless), for the children, for your appearance, your hair, the day of the week, for breathing . . .

Summing Up . . .

Developing knowledge both about yourself and your current situation is a vital step in the process of personal learning and development. It is both the place to begin and the place to return to as you assess and re-assess your progress and achievements.

Opening our minds to wider perspectives and new possibilities is crucial to our progress. We need to examine our ingrained attitudes, assumptions and beliefs about other people and view them as individuals rather than types.

And the same applies to how we see ourselves. If we can regard ourselves as unique, creative and talented, we are more likely to be able to tap into our own knowledge and wisdom. Gaining feedback from others can be helpful here, both in terms of the image we present to the world and the skills that other people see in us.

You don't have to be at your lowest ebb in order to be motivated to move forward, but circumstances of challenge and change can be highly motivating, not least because we often want to run away! Our motivation tends to follow a pattern or hierarchy, in which we strive to meet our most basic needs first - food, shelter and security. Once these needs have been met, we progress to other needs such as the need to belong, the need to achieve and ultimately, the need to fulfil ourselves. These higher order needs are about the quality and richness of our lives. We were made for more than survival.

Chapter 2

Where Past & Future Meet

*I know the solution. When we have a world of now, with no
shadows of yesterdays or clouds of tomorrow, then saying what we
can do will work.*
Goldie Ivener

- Out of the shadows
- Changing the script
- Your values, hopes and dreams
- One day my prince will come
- Action Points
- Summing up . . .

There's an antique shop in my local shopping centre
called *Whispers of the Past*. It's an appealing name
conjuring up images of fine furniture, china,
patchwork and lace, which is exactly what the shop
sells. We all live with whispers of our own past which
have brought us to where we are today. For many men
and women though, the past doesn't whisper. It
screams.

We cannot change the past. The only thing we can
change is our attitude towards it.

Reflecting on your personal history in terms of your
upbringing, education and childhood experiences, can
help you understand the factors which have shaped
your learning and development. For these influence
your expectations of what you can do, be and have in
the future.

Out Of The Shadows

Many people have cause to look back in anger and despair because their past still casts shadows over their lives. Tragically, there are some who live lesser lives without even realising they are reaping a legacy of their past.

Over the years, I have worked with many people whose personal histories have overwhelmingly dominated their current lives. Whatever their situation, they all had one thing in common. They had been overwhelmed by experiences which created barriers to their ability to live in the present and to stake a personal claim in the future.

It was as though the play of their life had already been written and they were acting out the script.

The most tragic was a young offender whose childhood had been spent in a succession of foster homes. Over a period of months in the prison where I met him, he became more and more withdrawn. His likeable, cheeky personality disappeared and in its place was a disturbed and troubled soul. His deteriorating behaviour gradually placed him beyond the reach of any kind of human warmth, to the extent that he retreated into some kind of isolated, impenetrable wasteland in his mind. When last I heard of him, he was alone in a punishment cell. I often wonder if he is still alive. The despair of his situation has never quite left me.

Changing The Script

By contrast, let me describe a friend and colleague who might have been overwhelmed by his past experiences, but chose not to be. It is a choice he continues to make every day as he re-writes the script of his own life, which was itself altered dramatically following a car crash almost 20 years ago . . .

At the age of 21, Ross Edwards was a keen sportsman and amateur footballer. He lived life to the full. One winter's evening, as he was giving other players a lift home after a match, the car he was driving slewed into a lamp post. All the passengers escaped unscathed. Ross was critically injured. For six weeks, he lay in a coma.

Over the ensuing months and years, he has travelled the long road to adjustment. He is physically challenged with impaired memory and concentration. Everyday living is a battleground on which personal dignity and pride is won or lost.

Fresh challenges

'I refuse to let my disability overwhelm me,' he asserts. 'It influences what I do and it informs the person I have become. But I refuse to play the role of helpless victim. It's a *different* life I have now. I'm not 'invalid'.'

'These years since my accident have been a learning process. I've learned about what really matters in my life: the value of family and friendship, the ability to take each day as it comes and the need to be listened to and taken seriously.

'Each day brings fresh challenges. I attend college, I take part in a prison visiting scheme and I'm a member of a support group for head-injured people and their families. The past is over and done with. I can't change it. But I can choose my own way forward. And that helps me get out of bed in the morning. I can write my own music.'

Do your past experiences *inform* your current life or *overwhelm* it? Have you managed to come to terms with your past experiences in a way that helps you move forward, or does your personal history dictate what you are and what you do?

A greater understanding of how you have become the person you are won't automatically enable you to move from being *overwhelmed* to *informed*, but it could be a powerful first step to taking control of your own life.

I remember visiting a women's prison and hearing from the Governor that a high proportion of the inmates had been victims of some sort of abuse. Some of them had gone from being abused to becoming abusers themselves. The tragedy is that these women couldn't or didn't 'change the script.'

Your Values, Hopes & Dreams

Our expectations of what we can achieve in the future will be, to a greater or lesser degree, influenced by our personal history. Other scripts come into play too, such as gender, class and culture. And we're all caught up in them. At the age of 17, I was invited to attend an interview for a place at Cambridge University. I was 'ordinary,' and didn't have the typical middle-class background or profile of a Cambridge student. I also knew that female places were thin on the ground, so they took only the most able girls. I didn't get offered a place - it wasn't in my script!

Being aware of our scripts and the way they influence us can help us develop independent values and goals which more truthfully reflect our personal aspirations.

Life, as my mum used to say, is not a rehearsal. Let's say you were to live to be 85 years old. This is:

* 1020 months
* 4420 weeks
* 31025 days

If you are already 40 years old, you have left:

- 540 months
- 2340 weeks
- 16425 days

One view of this is that the sands of time are running out. Another is that there are 16425 reasons to make every moment count. There is an inevitable tension between living out the day and planning for tomorrows that might never happen, especially if living out the day is painful and difficult. A state of distress can become a way of life, extending endlessly into the future. We then begin to ask: *What's it all for?* and it becomes a life without hope.

Thinking about what we value most in our lives can give us direction, by enabling us to concentrate on what we have consciously decided is important and meaningful. This may not change a difficult situation, but it can help us live with it, perhaps, in a more constructive way. Tension and uncertainty can be a spur to action, as explained more fully in Chapter 5.

One Day My Prince Will Come

If you kiss a toad, you don't get a prince - you get slime in the mouth and bad memories.
Laura Shlessinger

When I was young, I spent a lot of time day-dreaming. Hardly surprising really, since my reading diet comprised the Hans Christian Anderson and Brothers Grimm fairy tales along with The Knights of the Round Table. And then there was Disney. No wonder I used to give frogs a second glance.

No handsome prince hacked his way through a forest to kiss me awake after a hundred-year sleep, but I certainly woke up at the age of 15 when I discovered the more real delight of snogging on the back row of the cinema with Gary. We didn't live happily ever after, but I still have fond memories of the Odeon, though I can't quite remember what the film was!

Men have been fed the fairy tales too. The tough, handsome, strong, virile, macho all-action regular hero (a *must* for damsels in distress) has such a strong place in popular culture and so little to do with the reality of modern living and individual aspiration, it's no wonder that issues of gender and power create conflict and tension within every level and facet of society. Not quite 'happy ever after.'

Wish List

Hopes and dreams do not have to be fairy tale fantasy or based on the media hype that would have us dreaming of permanent youth, beauty, sex appeal and sunshine. Neither do your dreams have to capture the hearts and minds of nations or generations, or even your family - just you. They need to embrace the things and people you value and your own priorities.

Most of us have a vague idea of what we want for ourselves and those closest to us. Obviously this can change through time and circumstance. But for now and for starters, what would be your answers to the following:

- What do I want to *do* over the next 5 years?
- What do I want to *be* over the next 5 years?
- What do I want to *have* over the next 5 years?

Alternatively, think about your dream life or your dream job. Where are you? Who are you with? What are you doing? Is your dream in any way achievable? How could you make it happen?

Holistic dreams

We are whole, *rounded* people - mind, body and spirit. Hopes and aspirations which reflect these various dimensions of your life and enable you to achieve a sense of balance may be the kindest to yourself in the longer term, even if finding that balance can be a never-ending journey.

To be without hopes and dreams is a place of loss . . . loss of our birthright as a human being.
Anne Wilson Schaef

Action Points

- **Being different** - Think of someone you know who has deliberately chosen a lifestyle or work option which has required them to swim against the tide. Consider the personal qualities and determination which this will have required. How might this determination have arisen? Could there be lessons to learn here?

- **Visualise the future** - Who are the most important people in your life? Visualise yourself and them five years into your future. Create a positive, joyful image in your mind. What are you all doing? Where are you? How are you interacting? *What are the issues you need to take care of in the present, for this future to happen?*

- **Timeframes** - Consider how many hours of your waking time you spend in the various activities you do in a typical week. Perhaps you might keep a diary to record this and calculate the hours in portions according to areas of activity, such as work, leisure, family, education etc, whatever is appropriate for you. You could illustrate this information in a pie-chart like the one below. Then draw a second chart and divide it into portions which represent how you would *prefer* to allocate your time. In the two charts illustrated here, note how the proportions have changed in the Preferred example and that there is an extra area - 'me' time.

Examples

Current   Preferred

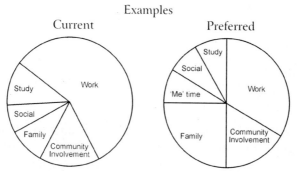

- **Impossible dream** - Identify a dream that is so far removed from where you are now that you can't imagine achieving it. Think about what would have to happen for this dream to become reality. At best, you might decide to break it down into goals which are achievable in some way; at worst, it will indicate some of your values. Either way, hang on to it.

- **Your life in your hands** - From the thinking you have done on your own hopes and dreams, can you now put them into short statements? The use of the words *I CAN* places the emphasis on yourself and your capability.

Eg I CAN learn to like myself more.
I CAN take responsibility for my own decisions.
I CAN retrain for a new career.
My main hopes for the future are that:

I CAN _____

I CAN _____

I CAN _____

Your responses to these Action Points can help you identify goals for the future. The process whereby you can plan ways of achieving them is included in Chapter 6.

Summing Up . . .

Whatever your background, situation or motivation, it is important to stake a claim in your own future by deciding what is important to you and what you want and hope for in the months and years ahead.

We all carry a variety of baggage from the past - some of it helpful, some of it inappropriate and some of it even harmful. It can make the difference between you being informed by your own past or overwhelmed by it. For those who feel they are in the latter category, take heart. You are obviously a survivor. Some of the strength, determination and insight which has brought you to this point in your life can help you move forward.

However turbulent or challenging the circumstances in your own past may have been, you can create a different life script from the one you have been handed, by taking control of your own life and 'writing your own music.'

This also involves creating a balance between the things you want to do and the things other people expect you to do and between the different dimensions of your life - mind, body and spirit.

Your hopes and dreams don't have to be based on fairy tales or the media hype which bombards us. They can be small dreams or big ones - anything that is meaningful for you and ties in with the people and things you most value in your life. Your dreams may change and that's fine too. Having one is what is important.

Chapter 3

Circles Of Your Life

Most people are on the world, not in it - have no conscious sympathy or relationship to anything about them - undiffused, separate and rigidly alone like marbles of polished stone, touching but separate.
John Muir

- Changing world views
- Your working world
- No more gold watches
- Competency counts
- Action Points
- Summing up . . .

Imagine you could propel yourself 30 years into the future and look back on our world as it is now. Is it conceivable that you might ask yourself any of the following?

- Did we really have separate banks and building societies?
- Did we really have 'phones connected to the wall by wires?
- Did we really have computer software that took six months to learn how to use?
- Did we really think we could carry on abusing the earth's resources at that rate?
- Did we really think farming was simply about producing food?
- Did we really think big organisations needed big offices?
- Did we really think the welfare state would support us from cradle to grave?

Changing World Views

In the same way that we can have experiences which shift the way we see things and open our minds to new possibilities, so can society in general. Even world views are open to challenge and change. The practice of science was at one time, for example, based on the belief that the Earth was the centre of the Universe. There was a time too when people believed the Earth was flat. Only when these beliefs were challenged, first by individuals, then by society collectively, could new possibilities and discoveries emerge.

You could argue that society, like the individuals within it, needs to be capable of change in order to progress, not only in response to new ideas and unfolding events, but also in anticipation of them. Our own age has seen change and transformation unequalled in pace and scale to any that has gone before. And our current understandings of the world we live in are still being challenged.

The future beckons

Key trends identified by John Naisbitt in his book *Megatrends* (Futura 1984) include the following shifts and changes, the full impact of which may still be to come:

* from a national economy to a world economy
* from an industrial society to an information society
* from centralisation to decentralisation
* from institutional help to self-help
* from hierarchies to networking

Against such a complex landscape, forging our personal futures with positive purpose creates the question *how wide is our world?* Do we close the doors, batten down the hatches, and stay safe inside a narrow world of care and concern for ourselves and our nearest and dearest, hoping against hope that nothing terrible happens to us and ours?

Or do we make a drop in the ocean more of a puddle, by taking a stand or making common cause with others to act collectively on our wider world?

Your Working World

The change from an industrial society to an information society has revolutionised the world of work. The main commodity of this information society is knowledge - the knowledge to design and deliver products and services that meet the market demand for continual improvement. This has created tremendous opportunities, but has also ushered in massive unemployment, particularly within the traditional blue-collar workforce.

Privatisation, market-testing and compulsory competitive tendering have also resulted in organisations having to become meaner, leaner and much more competitive than ever before. Businesses which formerly worked alongside each other as colleagues are now competitors in the market place. This applies in the voluntary sector as well as the private and public sectors. There are two types of organisation nowadays: the quick and the dead.

No More Gold Watches

If we try and define the older, traditional view of work alongside the current reality of work, it looks something like this:

The way we were	The way we are
Manufacturing focus	Service focus
Long hours	No job security
Stable work patterns	Flexible work patterns
'A job for life'	Short-term contracts
Permanent staff	Increase in use of part-time / temporary staff
Hierarchical organisation	Horizontal organisation
Promotion through age and seniority	Promotion across organisation through skill development in different roles
Large workforce covering all functions	Smaller core workforce - ancillary functions contracted out
Focus on status, specialisms and managerialism	Focus on competence, multi-skilling, flexibility and teamworking
Effort deserves reward	Work smarter as well as harder
Paid for time at work - inputs	Payment by results - outputs

The new reality

It's easy to deliver the platitude about welcoming change as an opportunity for growth. But given the pace and depth of organisational change and its impact on individuals, it can be difficult, if not well nigh impossible, to perceive delayering, restructuring, down-sizing (the friendly term is right-sizing), heavier work loads and the disappearance of traditional promotion paths and pay rises, as anything but a personal kick in the teeth. It's not fair. The new reality of work is not about fairness however, it's about the laws of supply and demand.

If you attend any kind of seminar or talk on the subject of organisational change, you're sure to be challenged with a quote such as:

Go on doing what you've always done and you wind up with the same as you've always had.

In fact, in the world of work, if you go on doing what you've always done, you can wind up with even less than you've always had, because your skills and working practices may be increasingly irrelevant and inappropriate to the commercial environment. The people who benefit from this avalanche of change are those with the appropriate knowledge, skill, and flexibility required in the market place.

A case in point

Rasshied's experience of life after redundancy was more positive than he expected . . .

'I had been head of the technical support team in a computer services company for five years when it was taken over. I didn't like the new manager and opted for redundancy. Then I panicked. I was 48 years old, with two children to support and a mortgage, so I knew the money wouldn't last long. I applied for lots of jobs without success.

'Then I spotted an advert in the paper offering free business start-up courses at the local business shop, so I went along and they encouraged me to think of becoming self-employed. It took ages to produce a business plan, but eventually I set up my own office at home, offering a 24-hour helpline and technical support to small businesses. I've never worked harder or longer than I do now, but it's great to be my own boss.'

This experience is in marked contrast to that of Sarah (36), a former administrative assistant with a civil service agency . . . 'I could see the writing was on the wall with the arrival of market testing. I chose voluntary redundancy because of the package, but I never thought I'd feel so low afterwards. I've picked up some temping, but I find that I'm barely adequate in modern office skills. I've lived a sheltered life, career-wise, and I need to consider further training.'

The main factor in Rasshied's success was the knowledge and skill he was able to apply and use for himself. Sarah was less able to move to another job, because she did not have the relevant skills required by other organisations.

Competency Counts

Organisations need knowledge to survive and prosper, but knowledge needs to be applied through performance. One of the key words used in organisations therefore is *competence*. A competence is not something you simply know, but the practical ability to apply your knowledge to a particular standard of performance, ie a measurable level of skill. Organisations are increasingly developing competency frameworks which define the types and levels of skills required to deliver their business.

If it moves, measure it

Many job descriptions now use action verbs such as: *organise, produce, design, compile, assemble, plan* and *calculate*. This is because they are quantifiable and measurable against targets. The idea is that all performance can be measured, even when it involves 'soft' targets such as customer care. This trend has produced all sorts of customer / client / patient charters, though cynics would say that much can be hidden in rhetoric.

In general, the competencies sought by all organisations include:

- teamworking
- building / maintaining relationships
- focusing on customer / client needs and requirements
- achieving results
- gathering / sharing information

Note how you could gain such competencies in many different types of work, paid or unpaid. They are all *transferable* in that you could apply them across different organisations.

Teamworking

There is a growing emphasis on teamworking because teams rather than individuals are the basic work unit within an organisation. Many teams are expected to manage themselves and be accountable for their performance. You may find it interesting to note the following areas of management competency, which in the past have been expected of individual managers alone. Increasingly now, employers prefer that each member of the team possesses skills in these areas. They include (as defined by the Management Charter Initiative):

- setting and prioritising objectives
- showing self-confidence and personal drive
- taking decisions
- managing personal learning and development
- monitoring / responding to actual against planned activities
- obtaining the commitment of others
- collecting and organising information
- showing concern for excellence

Action Points

- **A world in us** - Consider your *worlds* using the following prompts:

51

Your wider world: What are the social, economic, environmental and political issues about which you feel most concern / enthusiasm? If you could make a difference in one area, which would it be?

Your working world: Why do you work in your job? What are the most satisfying / frustrating parts of your work? Is stress at work a particular issue for you? If so, is it being created by the way the organisation is structured, by the organisational climate, or by the way people work and communicate with one another? Refer also to Chapter 8 Meeting Stress - An occupational hazard.

- **Make your mark** - Use your feelings of concern on wider issues to make your voice heard. *Do* something, whether it's going on a countryside march, engaging in community issues, joining Amnesty International, or taking up membership of a political party.

- **Maintain an up-to-date CV (Curriculum Vitae)** - Apart from being a necessary preparation for job applications, compiling and maintaining a current CV is very good for your confidence. Everyone can have one - you don't need to have been in paid employment. It is a record of your skills, experience and qualifications which you should update regularly. There are many different styles and it will be worth your while researching the most appropriate format for yourself.

- **Network** - Keep in touch with local employment trends and issues through personal contacts and reading the local press. It's estimated that up to 70% of job vacancies are not publicly advertised.

- **Become a lifelong learner** - Take advantage of any learning opportunities - within or outside work - to add to your skill base and strengthen your confidence and competence. Build up a 'portfolio' of skills which are flexible and transferable. If you are unemployed, you may be eligible to join various training projects which allow you to gain further qualifications and work experience, without loss of benefits.

Summing Up . . .

Whatever the view from your window on the world, claiming your own future challenges you to ride the storm of a complex and changing society.

World views, like individual views, are open to challenge and change in the light of experience. The worlds in which we operate - the society we live in, the environment we work in and the more intimate circles of our social and personal life - inevitably impact on each other.

In this country, for example, a rising divorce rate, a growth in the number of single-parent families and an increase in the average age of the population are changing the way employers recruit and develop the talent they need. In the world of work itself, the Industrial Revolution has given way to the Information Revolution, bringing about a sea-change in work patterns and practices which has in turn affected the social life of the communities we live in.

The main commodity of this new information society is knowledge rather than manual work. The people who benefit are those who align their knowledge, skills and talents with the demands of the market place and take responsibility for their own learning and development. We are all expected to be lifelong learners.

Chapter 4

Personally Yours

No one can make you feel inferior without your consent.
Eleanor Roosevelt

- Becoming OK
- Pedestals & doormats
- Give yourself a good talking to
- I am 'stroked' therefore I am
- Action Points
- Summing up . . .

Each of us is a unique combination of skills, qualities, experience, creativity and potential. For as long as we live, we can continue to grow in knowledge and understanding, both of ourselves and the world around us. How much we use and apply this learning to choose or change our future actions will be influenced by the way we see and value ourselves.

The more positive our self-concept, the more likely it is that we will be able to relate with others positively and learn and grow in relationship to others. The quality and variety of our social and intimate relationships are, therefore, a valuable source of learning about the type of person we are.

Becoming OK

Have you ever been in one of those situations when your confidence has been ripped to shreds by someone else's rudeness, when you've come away feeling like something that crawled out from under a stone? We've probably all been there. It's bad enough if it happens occasionally. It's tragic if it becomes the norm.

In hindsight, these situations often become understandable if not forgivable, because they say far more about the other person than they say about you. People act out of their own feelings of anger, fear and fragility, as well as out of joy, strength and self-confidence. Can any parent put their hand on heart and say that they've never shouted at the kids because of the mood they've been in rather than what the kids have done?

I'm OK you're OK

In all our personal relationships, we have the opportunity to act out of feelings of acceptance and respect - or not. We can explore this idea further with the model *I'm OK You're OK,* in the book of the same name by American psychiatrist Thomas Harris (Arrow 1995).

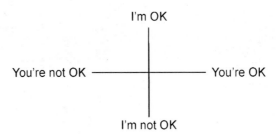

The way the grid works is to pair up all four options, which Harris terms *life positions,* and compare them as possible ways in which individuals can relate to each other.

Pedestals & Doormats

Consider the ways in which the following people might talk and behave:

- a person who thinks *they're not OK but others are OK*
- a person who thinks *they're OK but others are not OK*
- a person who thinks *they're not OK and nor are others*
- a person who thinks *they're OK and others are too*

In general, people who lack confidence or who don't feel good about themselves (*not OK*) will tend to be quite negative and reactive, whereas people who are comfortable and confident within themselves (*OK*) will tend to be positive and proactive. Your position and approach may change, however, according to the person you're dealing with and the situation.

Imagine you are the 'I' in these one-to-one relationships . . .

I'm not OK, You're OK - you don't feel good about yourself in this relationship (or *any* relationship?) Your self-confidence is on the floor. Maybe you have put your partner on a pedestal, or become totally dependent through attitude or circumstance. Unfortunately, doormats get trodden on. You may say things like: *I don't know what I would do without you . . . You're so wonderful . . . I'm so lucky to have you.* While this situation may suit both partners for a while, this may change. The doormat might become more assertive or the *OK* partner might becomes *less OK*, perhaps through poor health or demotion.

I'm OK, you're not OK - you feel great about yourself, but you look down on your partner. You are unlikely to listen to them or value their opinion, unless perhaps it reflects your own. You may be aggressive towards them, but equally, you could be patronising or over-protective. You may say things like: *I told you so . . . Don't you know anything? . . . Trust me, I know best dear.* This can create resentment from the *not OK* partner which ultimately erupts in aggressive behaviour.

I'm not OK, You're not OK - you're both on a downward spiral with this one. This is not an understanding born of shared fragility, but abject despair. This relationship devalues both partners through a denial of trust, responsibility and hope. You may say things like: *What's the point? . . . Why should we bother? . . . Nothing will make any difference . . .*

I'm OK, You're OK - you're onto a winner here. Your awareness of your own and your partner's strengths enables you to develop a mutually satisfying relationship based on shared trust and respect. This is the recipe for long-term relationships. You may say things like: *Let's do it! . . . Life is for living . . . Shall we plan . . . Let's work it out . . .*

At home and at work

You can apply this model to other relationships, including those at work. The positions of *I'm not OK, You're OK* and *I'm OK, You're not OK* are commonly played out in the working environment, especially in hierarchical organisations, where power and status equate with being *OK* and lack of power and status equates with being *not OK.* You can also use this model alongside the idea of *Parents, Adults and Children* explained in Chapter 10. Teamworking is a current trend that cuts across these dynamics of power in favour of a focus on competence.

Give Yourself A Good Talking To

Being able to feel *more OK* about ourselves and others requires us to challenge the attitudes and assumptions learned through our childhood or culture which undermine us, eg:

- *I'm weak*
- *I'm a victim*
- *Other people know best*
- *I shouldn't make a fuss*
- *The others won't like it if I seem too clever*
- *Nice girls don't do that / Big boys don't cry*
- *Don't be pushy*
- *If you can't take the heat, get out of the kitchen*

Some of these messages are familiar gender stereotypes, but they can still be damaging. I speak as someone who was told by her mother, at the age of 13, that it might not be wise to beat the boys at snooker in case it hurt their male pride. This didn't worry me particularly, because my snooker wasn't that hot. But tennis was something else!

We are what we *think*, so turn those negative messages into positive statements which affirm you, rather than constrain you. Here are some examples of affirmations to help knock on the head any remaining feelings of learned helplessness you may be harbouring:

- I am strong, I have value
- I do not need to stay a victim
- I have the ability to solve my own problems
- I'm proud of who and what I am
- I can acknowledge the past and leave it behind
- I can enrich my own life

I Am 'Stroked' Therefore I Am

- *My father never praises me when I do something right. But he's always the first to criticise when I do something wrong.*
- *We only hear from our manager if one of us makes a mistake. Then he hits the roof.*
- *I hated school. All I remember is teachers shouting at me for being slow.*

These experiences are not uncommon.

Our personal relationships thrive on the expression of positive regard - the *I'm OK, You're OK* position. But how many of us receive positive recognition of ourselves on a regular basis? We all need to be *stroked* regularly, psychologically speaking, to feel good about ourselves and perform well.

Stroke theory was popularised by psychiatrist Dr Eric Berne in his bestselling book *Games People Play* (Penguin 1970). A stroke is a unit of recognition - whether words, looks or physical gestures - from one person to another. The need we have as children to be held, cuddled and stroked in order to develop properly, so the theory goes, continues through our adult lives. Such is our need to be recognised that even strokes which are negative, such as being criticised, can be regarded as better than none at all. A complete absence of strokes denies our existence. This is one reason why adults, as well as children, may resort to bad behaviour to get attention.

Better by far, however, are positive strokes regularly given and received, which denote warm, caring appreciation and approval. Perhaps we all get far fewer positive strokes than we need, to flourish as we might.

I remember a conversation with a long-term prisoner who had been in solitary confinement. This had obviously removed any strokes from his environment. The prisoner spoke of the intense fear he felt when he was eventually being moved back to his own cell and he met two other prisoners in the corridor. They posed no threat. But having been deprived of human contact for a time, his perceptions had changed and he described the other prisoners as double-decker buses, which he was convinced were going to run over him. He described solitary confinement as 'brain damage.'

How long since you stroked your partner or the significant others in your personal world?

Kind words may be short and easy to speak but their echoes are truly endless.
Mother Theresa

Action Points

- **OK?** - Think about the situations in which you feel *OK* and *not OK* about yourself and others. Identify situations of personal conflict or difficulty and try to work out the life position being adopted by the other party in relation to you. Does your own position contribute to the conflict?

- **Your stroke balance** - List five important people in your life. Next to each name, place a score out of 5 (with 5 the best) which corresponds with the amount of positive recognition and support you give them on a regular basis. Then score *them* according to the amount of stroking they give you. How is the stroke balance? Are you constantly affirming your partner, children, boss, friends etc and receiving mere morsels in return? Is it the other way round? Or 5-all in each case? Equal stroking tends to be indicative of a happy relationship. If the strokes are completely out of balance and this is typical, it may be a sign of difficulty or anxiety within the relationship which merits further attention

- **Still here, still learning** - Think of something you have learned how to do recently that you didn't know how to do five years ago (sky-diving, tackling your mother-in-law, conversational Spanish?). Then think of something you knew how to do five years ago, but couldn't have done five years earlier. Keep going if you want! Does this illustrate how you have always been learning?

- **'I' for impact** - Declare your own identity - your feelings, experiences and learning, by writing a page of 'I' statements. This is a very powerful way of defining yourself and is included here by popular request! Begin by completing these statements in any style you like, but don't stop there: *I am* _____, *I will* _____, *I hope* _____, *I have* _____, *I like* _____ etc.

- The following example was compiled by Jane Gallacher, whose story features in the next chapter, so you can read these powerful statements between the lines of her life:

- *I am* a survivor!

- *I am* like a river with twists and turns but always flowing.

- *I've* been up and I've been down and I've certainly been around!

- *I am* on a journey, but the destination isn't as important as the travelling.

- *I have* learned to take one step at a time and believe in myself.

- *I like* the feel of the sun on my face and warm earth on my fingers - maybe I'm a snail!

- *I have* an old soul and wisdom I've never been told.

- *I will* carry on learning and moving on, for I have high ambitions.

- *I hope* I can live up to them!

- **What kind of traveller are you?** - Personal development is a journey of discovery. Take a few minutes to think of the kind of traveller you are: intrepid, no holds barred, or hesitant, needing to take a few steps at a time? You may want to travel alone or with others, slowly or quickly, carrying lots of baggage or none. However you travel, it is important to know the resources you have with you in terms of assets, talents and skills and also the type of support you can call on when the going gets tough.

Summing Up . . .

How you feel about yourself is crucial to how you grow and develop and also to how you relate with other people. Positive, confident people usually enjoy positive relationships, whilst people who feel inadequate or vulnerable often experience difficulties in their dealings with others.

The *I'm OK You're OK* model, which illustrates the various life positions people adopt in their relationships, is a useful one to help us define those situations in which we feel confident and comfortable and those in which we feel vulnerable or unhappy. It can also throw light onto situations of conflict at home and at work.

Being able to feel *more OK* requires you to challenge your own negative messages and give yourself a good talking to, in terms of positive internal dialogue. Carry the thought, for example, that you are doing the best you can with what you currently know. And you are learning all the time. When you know more, you will do even better!

We all benefit too from being stroked, psychologically speaking, in the sense of receiving positive recognition from others. Because of our need for such human acknowledgement, we may even prefer being criticised or shouted at, to being totally ignored.

Personal development is about travelling on a journey of discovery - of self and the world around you. The author and activist Maya Angelou talks about three types of traveller in her book *Even The Stars Look Lonesome* (Virago 1998). The first is the person who prepares meticulously for their journey and all eventualities; the second, the person who is more timid and may even return home should they meet obstacles along the way, and the third, 'the desperate traveller,' the category in which she places herself, the person whose only certain destination is somewhere other than where they've been.

Part Two

Know Your Potential

Chapter 5

Creating Choices

*If you think you can, you can. And if you
think you can't, you're right.*
Mary Kay Ash

- Defying the odds
- Mountain men and valley boys
- Building personal power
- Choices and self-esteem
- Starting from a position of strength
- Action Points
- Summing up . . .

Defying The Odds

It's quite a thought, but *you* represent the total of all
the choices you have made in your life. And you can
build a different future for yourself by creating fresh
choices.

Exercising your choices is not always an easy option. It
can be a continuing act of defiance against personal
circumstances.

Jane Gallacher's story takes most of us into uncharted
territory. The youngest of six children, she lived with
her grandparents until the age of 4 . . .

'My first memory is the horror of my gran collapsing
and dying in the house with only me there. Family life

for me after that was being shuttled around friends and relatives with my brothers and sisters. I went to 10 different primary schools. We had bursts of time at home, but mum wasn't stable. She'd disappear regularly and dad, when he came in drunk, would have us walking the streets - all these kids and a dog - sometimes all night, because he didn't want us in the house. Social Services didn't come near us.

'My schooling was a nightmare. I looked like a poor soul so it's not surprising I was bullied. Then at 17, I married a man who became violent and abusive. We had two children and the abuse destroyed our family life. Eventually I took the kids and left. We struggled by in hostels and refuges, but life was chaotic and the kids became very troubled. I made the heart-rending decision that they should go into care.

'This was a turning point. As I started to recover from the trauma that was my life, I decided not to let my past become my future. Now, years later, I have a home, friends and a job, and I see my kids regularly. Finally, after being to hell and back, I understand that I deserve to have choices and rights just like everyone else. My world can still be frightening, but it also holds hope and promise. That's every child's birthright really isn't it?'

Oh you're so predictable!

You may be familiar with the story of the Russian scientist Pavlov and his experiments with dogs. Every time Pavlov fed a group of dogs, he would ring a bell so that the dogs associated the sound of the bell with being fed. Eventually they would salivate at the sound of the bell alone. They had become so conditioned, that their response was automatic.

Do we develop automatic responses to people and situations or do we separate the stimulus from the response (the bell from the salivating!) which allows us to *choose* how we will react? If, for instance, someone says something to us which makes us angry, do we automatically hit back with bitter words or maybe retreat predictably into an injured silence? It can be helpful to question some of the behaviours we have adopted out of habit, especially if these behaviours take away our choices and make us victims of circumstance.

Are any of the following phrases familiar?

- *It's not my fault*
- *She / he made me do that*
- *I can't help it - it's in the genes / it's the way I am*
- *It's more than my job's worth*
- *My wife / husband / partner / boss doesn't understand me . . .*

These typically reactive responses infer that we don't have any choice. But you don't *have* to blame other people for your toothache, lack of job satisfaction, affair with the next-door neighbour . . . however convenient. If someone kicks you, you don't automatically have to kick back, as I tell my teenage son, before he repays his younger sister in kind!

It can make us feel better to shift the responsibility for our behaviour onto other people, especially if we feel they are at fault. But taking responsibility for our actions is more helpful in the long run, because it builds our capability and confidence.

I recently met a man who is serving a long prison sentence for a crime he believes he was 'fitted up' for. A lengthy appeals process has gone against him and he has been in a state of extreme mental anguish. The choice he has left, is how he deals with this situation. After considerable effort, he has decided that he will survive. His way forward is to take each day at a time and work out some of his energy and frustration in the prison gym.

Taking responsibility for things we can do something about and exercising the choices available to us - even if they are limited - is a useful strategy, because it develops our ability to deal with life. Making choices carries an element of risk, but this includes the risk of success as well as failure.

Mountain Men And Valley Boys

The advertising industry use the saying:
Are you a mountain man or a valley boy?

In other words, are you the sort of person who has the courage and daring to leap into the unknown, or do you prefer to stay safe in familiar territory?

The advertising industry, in common with our culture in general, applauds the mountain men - those individuals willing to take tremendous risks in pursuit of great achievement.

But where does that leave the valley boys? At the foot of the mountain feeling guilty?

Or safe and warm at home by the fire, counting their blessings?

We are all different in how we assess and accept various levels of risk and let's be honest, risk is scary. Nevertheless, a willingness to risk change is a healthy attitude to develop, because it helps us deal with the results of the decisions we make and the changes or crises that happen to us out of the blue.

Thinking about your own attitude to risk is worthwhile. It gives you knowledge about how you learn, what you fear, and particularly, the way you make plans. Your answers to the following questions will indicate whether you need security, and may therefore prefer a low-risk approach to personal planning, or whether you thrive on challenge and like to pursue a higher-risk approach.

- Do you find security in consistency of lifestyle, job, relationships etc?
- Do you often dream about having your life over again and doing things differently?
- Has your previous experience of taking risks been positive or negative?
- Do you view your mistakes as examples of incompetence or as learning experiences?
- Do you worry a lot about what other people think?
- Does your approach to life and work allow for changes of direction?
- Will the people closest to you support you to change and develop?

It's easier to take risk in your stride if you have a healthy level of self-esteem and a sense of your *personal power*, so let's look now at what this means.

Building Personal Power

Power has all sorts of connotations: *power struggle, power politics, power dressing, lust for power* etc. Power obviously comes in a wide range of colours, shapes and sizes. The dictionary definition is the ability *to do, to act or to influence*, so let's concentrate on that, because it's about making things happen.

Brute strength can, of course, make things happen. So can money, information, rank and status. Power without the exercise of personal responsibility can lead to abuse, illustrated in the saying: *Power tends to corrupt, absolute power corrupts absolutely* (Lord Acton). But power and responsibility *together* is a winning combination for personal effectiveness. As a society and as individuals we have the choice . . .

A case for treatment

On a recent hospital visit, I was struck by the casual indignities endured in helpless silence by the elderly patients in the ward - the patronising use of *we* (as in 'have *we* been to the toilet yet?'); the barely-disguised impatience of the consultant on his ward round, and the insensitivity of nursing staff who left a sleeping patient lying on her bed inappropriately covered, as the world and his wife strolled past at visiting time.

By what right do we disempower those who already feel the loss of health, strength and dignity which often accompanies the ageing process?

The power to choose

To be *empowered*, we need:

- knowledge and information
- a conscious awareness of personal power and motivation
- to be able to choose from a range of options
- to be able to tackle challenge and change
- to take personal responsibility for our actions

What's your power base?

There are three basic types of power:

Role power is the ability to influence others because of the role you adopt. A parent has this power over a child, a manager over a junior employee, a teacher over a pupil. We've all seen this power used and abused and many of us have been on both ends of it. I knew I'd lost it when my answer to a stroppy student's questioning of my interpretation of *Braveheart* was that I had a history degree and he hadn't. I also remember, at the age of 10, being aware that my own teacher lost respect when she threw a wooden blackboard rubber at a fellow pupil for saying that the opposite of clean was 'mucky.'

Expert power is the ability to influence others because of your expertise, knowledge or skill. This type of power generates respect regardless of status or role.

Resource power is the ability to give (or not) your various personal resources, including time, information, money, energy, knowledge, equipment and commitment.

Even if you lack other forms of power, you have personal resources in abundance.

Choices And Self-Esteem

If there's one thing guaranteed to boost, deplete or sabotage your personal power and choices, it's your level of self-esteem. No one gets it right all the time, but a healthy level of self-esteem - and the confidence it breeds - will let you get on with the business of living without being plagued by self-doubt.

Building self-esteem is a do-it-yourself job. It's great to be appreciated, but don't make others' opinions a barometer of your self-worth - it's not an exact science! Doing it yourself is the only option - through effort, perseverance and *action*. It's like placing so many bricks in a wall and making that wall higher and stronger. The action points in this book will give you a start. But open your mind to what your other bricks might be. Some of mine are:

- being open to new perceptions of myself and others
- developing positive relationships
- being assertive
- knowing when / how to get support
- setting realistic goals
- valuing my skills
- trusting in my ability to solve problems

Be aware that the bricks in your wall can be dislodged, damaged or destroyed by other people or events and that all of them are vulnerable to erosion and weathering. If the foundation course is firm however, it is easier to repair and rebuild when required. Could any of the bricks listed here be part of *your* foundation course?

Starting From A Position Of Strength

If you set yourself up for success, you will succeed.

This calls for a careful assessment of everything you've got going for you - personal qualities, skills, experience and resources and ways of using them to make an impact on your wider world. Compile your own list, preferably with feedback from friends and colleagues.

If you have a tendency to underestimate your skills (join the club), consider the tasks you undertake in your various roles. For example, a person who runs a home and cares for children will use a wide range of task-based and people-based skills, including:

- prioritising tasks
- gathering / communicating information
- listening
- developing / maintaining personal relationships
- food handling and preparation
- planning and budgeting
- time management

All of these skills are transferable into other roles and other environments. No one is *just* a housewife.

If you want to move forward in terms of work or training, various skills audits are available from careers advice services, who also have information about local opportunities. You may be offered a computer analysis which suggests career ideas. *Bingo-caller* was one of the suggestions for me, I remember, but it was further down the list than *journalist!*

The process of setting goals, described in the next chapter, will help you define some options and

actions. It doesn't matter how small your steps are. What does matter is that you take some.

Begin by finding out what you're good at and do more of it.

Action Points

*   **Winning ways** - Being able to *win* is important to your self-esteem, so build definitions of success which encourage you. Complete at least three statements:
    To me, success means _____
    To me, success means _____
    To me, success means _____
    (Eg being able to run my own business, finding / changing employment, being more assertive etc)

*   **SWOT yourself** - An analysis of Strengths, Weaknesses, Opportunities and Threats is a planning

tool for individuals and organisations. Often represented as a grid of four boxes, Strengths and Weaknesses have an internal or personal focus, whilst Opportunities and Threats help you look outwards to external factors.

Strengths	Weaknesses
Opportunities	Threats

You should by now have a good idea of your strengths. Include aspects of your personal power, particularly your resource power.

- Weaknesses are often gaps in skills or experience.
- Opportunities can come from building on strengths or addressing weaknesses.
- Threats are factors which could undermine your opportunities.

- **Shelve the 'shoulds'** - We limit ourselves with rules about what we *should* or *shouldn't* do, eg I *should* always put other people first; I *should* offer to take work home etc. This implies we would be wrong if we did things differently. If, for *should,* you substitute *could*, it gives you a choice . . .
  - I *could* always put others first.
  - I *could* offer to take work home.

- **Power gauge** - Explore your power to act within a difficult or stressful situation.
  What are your choices? Can you opt out or leave? Can you change the situation? Can you change your attitude towards it? Can you influence others to act?
  - What *can you* do to change the outcome?
  - What *can you* choose to feel about it?
  - What *can you* work towards doing in the future?
  - What support *can you* enlist?

Summing Up . . .

This chapter has emphasised the importance of recognising and using your personal power to create choices.

Being empowered involves a conscious awareness of your ability to do, to act and to influence. It also means taking responsibility for what you do, however tempting or convenient it may be to pass the buck.

You can exercise power through your roles, your skills and particularly your resources, such as time, energy, money and determination. Recognising your power in all its aspects and abundance, however challenging your circumstances, and building your own self-esteem, will help you move forward from a position of strength.

Power can oppress as well as enable. We are all capable of using our power to oppress others, not just in the physical sense, but by taking away other people's choices - even with the best of intentions. Equally, we have probably all felt disempowered at various points in our lives. Reflecting on your own experiences will help you evaluate how effectively you use your personal power just now.

'We would rather you didn't ask for any assistance with dressing or toileting during staff hand-over times,' explained the harassed care assistant to the disabled resident. 'And meal times are difficult because we're very busy. But never forget that this is your home.' Power - there's nothing quite like it.

Chapter 6

Making Things Happen

A journey of a thousand miles begins with a single step.

- Climbing to new heights
- Journeys and destinations
- Yes but . . .
- Be SMART
- 'Just do it'
- Action Points
- Summing up . . .

Climbing To New Heights

Kieron MacKenzie is a mountain man. His goal is the size of Everest, all 29028 feet of it, which he aims to climb to celebrate the Millennium - and his 40th birthday.

It takes considerable planning and not a little practice, which is how we met - Kieron in his climbing gear, looking ready to scale the highest mountain in the world, and me, stylish in a cloud of white fur, dressed as a rabbit.

I should perhaps add here that we were both participating in the launch of his New Heights Millennium Challenge in front of thousands of Edinburgh shoppers, by taking part in an eight-hour team *walk* - the equivalent height of Everest - using gymnasium step machines and raising money for charity. Hence the rabbit.

This veteran of famous peaks, including Mount
Kilimanjaro in Tanzania and Mount McKinley in
North America, has no hesitation about following his
dream to the top of the world, and no illusions about
the hazards and hardships he faces. His physical
preparation will include trips to Nepal and South America
climbing peaks in excess of 23000 feet. The mental
preparation has already begun . . . 'I visualise a lot. I
have climbed Everest a few times in my head already.'
He continues: 'I suppose I am someone who has a spirit
of adventure. I like to have goals to work towards. But
I don't describe myself as an excellent climber, perhaps
slightly above average. I want to demonstrate that you
don't have to be super-fit or superhuman to do things.'

Kieron admits to feeling fear sometimes. 'There's a lot of risk assessment going on and fear is part of that. It's all calculated. I have a healthy respect for what I do.'

Self-reliance

Although he will make the climb as part of a team expedition, there's a huge emphasis on self-reliance. 'I want to get to the summit. That may or may not happen. I obviously want to prepare as much as possible to make that happen. I focus on the goal more than anything and the journey itself is part of the goal.'

Kieron's attempt on Everest is being sponsored by local businessmen and is expected to generate thousands of pounds for charity. Meanwhile, in his quieter moments away from his expanding sportswear retail business, he finds time to learn to play the guitar. He smiles. 'It's a more relaxed method of gaining new skills.'

Journeys And Destinations

Some people have a clear idea of where they are going and how they plan to get there. Others set out like Maya Angelou's 'desperate travellers,' certain only about their need to move on to a place other than where they've been.

Ways of learning

Whichever kind of traveller you are, the journey you take is a many-splendoured learning process:

- *We learn by experience.* We *plan* things, *do* things and *reflect* on what happens as a result. If something works for us, we probably do it again. If it doesn't work for us, we may try something different.

- *Our learning in one area impacts on other areas.* Eg if you learn to be more assertive at work, you will sooner or later find yourself being more assertive at home too.

- *No learning is wasted.* I learned the truth of this from a 35-year-old client who had been a user of mental health services since his teens. His efforts to make a fresh start were about denying those painful years, but since this comprised all his adult life, it proved an impossible task. It was only when he began to explore the enormous knowledge and understanding he had gained through his experiences, that his way forward became clearer. He now works successfully as a volunteer advocate for clients with mental health problems and this has given him the confidence to return to college.

Travelling hopefully

Whether we learn by gradually pushing out our parameters of awareness and experience, or by suddenly breaking out of our comfort zone, we have to move away from the familiar and the known. As the proverb says:

You cannot discover new oceans
unless you have the courage to lose sight of the shore.

Your destination is, of course, important - and the rest of this chapter is about helping you define and reach your goals. But don't underestimate the *process* of travelling and learning. It is this which affords you glimpses of your own potential and allows you to create common currency with others through your personal exploration of your own fragility and power.

Yes But . . .

Many of us are equipped with self-destruct buttons. *Yes buts* are the reasons we create to convince ourselves we will fail. And if we succeed despite these, we then invent more *yes buts* as reasons why our achievement should not be recognised and celebrated. Oh for the power of positive thinking.

My colleague Pat has this down to a fine art:

'Yes, I suppose I could go on that computer course, but I'll probably be the oldest there and definitely the slowest,' she groaned.

Some time later, having successfully completed the course and made new friends among her fellow students . . . 'Yes, it was nice to get a merit for my module, but the tutor must have taken pity on me.'

Risk assessment

It is natural to have fears about stepping into the unknown. They simply need to be assessed for what they are, rather than grow arms and legs in the wild imaginings of your mind. This risk-assessment formula can be a useful way of managing the issue.

- Work with the fear. Explore it. *What am I afraid of?*
- Look at the worst scenario. *What's the worst that could happen?*
- Identify your support. *What's my safety net?*
- Balance the benefits and concerns. *Do the benefits outweigh the concerns?*

Reward yourself

If you expect too much of yourself, or fail to recognise your successes for what they are, you devalue your own efforts and risk destroying your motivation. Be aware that you can re-assess and re-set your goals if they prove either too challenging or not challenging enough. Be wary of putting all your eggs in one basket, or all your efforts into one outcome. Whatever the result, turn your *yes buts* into *yes ands*, and reward yourself for effort as well as for success.

If my colleague Pat were to use *yes and*, the result might be more positive . . . 'Yes, it was nice to get a merit for my module *and* I'm going to frame the certificate!'

Be SMART

However you categorise your goals, you will find it easier to turn them into reality if you break them down into smaller goals or milestones. Big or small, your actions should be SMART: Specific, Measurable, Achievable, Relevant and Time-bound.

*   *Specific*: Specify your actions. Eg if your goal is to be able to run your own business: where would you be doing this? What service / product would you be selling? Who would be your customers / competitors?

*   *Measurable*: How will you know that you are achieving your goal? You need to be able to measure your progress so you can alter your course if necessary. This is why splitting your goal into smaller objectives is useful.

- *Achievable*: Set your goals according to your current motivation, capability and situation. Don't make them dependent on other people, or circumstances which are not under your control.

- *Relevant*: Make your goals meaningful for you.

- *Time-bound*: Define when you're going to take action. Set yourself deadlines, but remember that Rome wasn't built in a day!

'Just Do It'

The only way to make things happen is to take action, or as the Nike sportswear slogan reminds us: *Just do it*. Use the goal-setting chart suggested here or make up your own. The act of defining your goals and writing them down encourages you to commit yourself and commitment is everything. Ordinary people committed to their goals are capable of doing extraordinary things. Talent by itself is no predictor of success.

You can set goals which are simple or ambitious. You can plan a trip to the theatre or a trip around the world. Use the thinking you have already done about your hopes, dreams, values and priorities. Visualise your goal like Kieron MacKenzie climbing Everest in his head. Create a picture in your mind of what it would be like to get there. What would it look like, sound like and feel like?

Drivers and resistors

Whatever the nature of your goals, there will be factors which can help or hinder your progress. The unexpected may hit you between the eyes, but at least you can attempt to manage the predictable.

Decide what forces are working for you (*drivers*) and what are working against you (*resistors*). You can move yourself forward by strengthening your drivers or reducing the resistors.

John used this idea to help him think through his goal of changing career at the age of 50. His drivers were: desire to leave job as a pensions administrator which he felt he'd outgrown, 'people' skills, no family responsibilities, some training qualifications and good references. His resistors: no clear career alternative, financial insecurity and anxiety about his age.

Since the drivers were already strong factors in helping him move forward, John paid attention to his resistors and set his first milestone as exploring alternative work options. He continued his job, but on a part-time basis, and became a volunteer with a national charity, working in training and development. Within months, he was offered paid employment with them.

Key success factors

Key success factors are things that must be in place for you to achieve your goal. If I want to learn Spanish, for example, key success factors would be the availability of a class or tutor, and my money, time and effort. Having defined these, I can assess my ability to control each, to maximise my chances of achievement. The more complex or ambitious your goal, the more thorough you need to be. *You*, ultimately, are the key to your own success.

MY GOAL	MY ACTIONS TO ACHIEVE IT (SMART)	DRIVERS	RESISTORS	KEY SUCCESS FACTORS
Learn conversational Spanish (Prior to extended visit to Spain in eight months' time)	Contact local college about evening class/ get prospectus - today. Ask partner to look after kids so I can attend - as soon as know day and time. Find out cost/set money aside - plan now. Look in library for books about Spain, its language and culture - next week.	Easy to get to college. Enjoy learning. Spanish trip coming up. Time to self is great.	Time pressures - kids quite demanding. Partner not always available. Money's tight.	Availability of class. I can get to it (need to find child care back-up). Money to pay for it. My time (must set aside time to practise in addition to class). My own motivation.
Adopt a more relaxed approach to life. I will have achieved this when: I feel less stressed. I shout less at the kids. I have some time to myself. I do things one at a time. I rush around less I become less irritable (and irritating!).	Talk to my partner/family about my goal and my need to have time to myself - do this now. Set time aside for each child separately to listen to them - over next week, regularly thereafter. Plan a list of treats for me - now. Take more exercise - swim every week - start Thursday. Plan a weekend break - soon! Prioritise my tasks better - make a list. Do less, delegate more - now. Do things more slowly - start now. Buy relaxation tape - weekend.	Feel better. Think more clearly. Have/be more fun. Better relationships. More energy. Achieve more.	Guilt, guilt, guilt!	My ability to deal with my own guilt at not meeting others' expectations. Need to maintain open communication with kids. Be willing for partner to have time to self too. My determination to keep time to myself even when others would fill it.

MY GOAL	MY ACTIONS TO ACHIEVE IT (SMART)	DRIVERS	RESISTORS	KEY SUCCESS FACTORS

Action Points

- **Practise being positive** - Commit yourself to what you want in your life, rather than what you don't want. Goals that you can work *towards* rather than away from, will give you a greater feeling of optimism and hope.

- **Seek support** - Seek out the company of people who will support you rather than add to your supply of *yes buts,* or, even worse, come out with *I told you so* if it all goes pear-shaped. It's easier to take risks if you have a solid network of personal support.

- **Work to best effect** - There is a theory about cause and effect called the Pareto principle (named after an Italian economist) which says that most effects are created by a few causes. Eg 80% of books are bought by 20% of the public; 80% of bus / rail passengers are carried on 20% of the routes; 80% of beer drunk is consumed by 20% of the population. *And 80% of your most productive work comes from 20% of your activity.* So consider what you achieved yesterday, or last week, or last year and ask yourself what was the 20% that delivered 80% of the results? Could some of your success derive from focusing on priorities and goals?

- **Become a problem solver** - Stay on target to achieve your goals by learning to deal with problems and difficulties. When you meet a problem:
  - *Define it - what* happened, *when* and *how?*
  - *Ask yourself Why?* If necessary, ask yourself 20 times, in order to get to the less obvious causes.
  - *Balance the solution with the perceived cause.* If the solution doesn't deal with the problem, you have either got a wrong (or partial) solution, *or* you need to reconsider the cause.

- *Take action.* If the cause or the solution is beyond your direct power to control, assess your power to *influence* the outcome yourself or with others.

- **Re-frame failure** - At some point you will fail, but this doesn't mean that you have to define yourself by failure or be overwhelmed by it. The most important thing about failure is how you respond to it. It can have a tremendous value in helping you analyse success, especially if you concentrate on what you *gained most* and what you might do differently *next time*. Recognise too, the value of inner as well as outer success. Maintaining inner confidence and resolve in the face of extreme challenge or disaster is a positive outcome.

Summing Up . . .

It is the process of goal-setting which translates our hopes and dreams into reality. Ordinary people committed to their goals achieve extraordinary things. As Scottish climber Kieron MacKenzie says: 'I want to demonstrate that you don't have to be super-fit or superhuman to do things.'

Any voyage of discovery involves moving away from the safety of the familiar. Assessing the risks, working out beforehand the forces that are working for you (drivers) and those working against you (resistors), and encouraging yourself by curbing any impulse to press your own self-destruct buttons, will allow you to set off confidently. Value the process of travelling - however rough the terrain!

Defining goals and milestones which are SMART (Specific, Measurable, Achievable, Relevant and Time-bound) and writing them down will help you commit to them and 'just do it.'

Can't is a four-letter word, asserts the advertising billboard featuring another climber, this time a wheelchair user, ascending a rock face. Commitment wins again.

Part Three

Know The Challenges You Face

Chapter 7

Meeting Change

To everything there is a season and a time for every purpose under heaven.
Ecclesiastes ch. 3 v.1

- In the event . . .
- Personal responses
- Just passing through
- Pain and gain
- On hurt and healing
- Action Points
- Summing up . . .

We live in a world of constant change in which we too change, develop, grow up and grow old. The poster in the advice centre summed it up:

Life - the great emotion picture

The pattern of our life is shaped by changing relationships, changing places, changing jobs and changing contrasts - joy and sorrow, fragility and power, hurt and healing. But the *perspective* is our own. For some, it's a case of *Life's a bitch and then you die.* Oscar Wilde was a tad more optimistic: *We are all in the gutter, but some of us are looking at the stars.*

Whatever perspective we usually take, we all experience events - positive and negative - which challenge our way of looking at life.

In The Event . . .

For as long as I can remember, I have known I was
adopted. My parents talked about it openly and when
I was 16, gave me a sad letter my natural mother had
sent them when I was 'handed over.' I valued it as a
tiny fragment of her.

I grew up with my adoptive older sister. We had a normal
happy childhood and our progress through adolescence
was punctuated with schoolwork, church choir, youth
club, boyfriends, parties, and in my case, pink hair!
Such was the foundation of my life from which I
moved on to college and career, marriage and family.

Opening the floodgates

I was already over 30, with two children of my own,
when mum 'phoned one evening to say that a contact
had been made regarding my natural mother. Whoosh!
The thoughts flooded in - curiosity about this woman,
concern about my parents, but mainly, the feeling that
I was on an express train to destination unknown. In
the space of five minutes, I felt like a different person.

A short while later, in a letter, in a 'phone call, in a
visit, in an instant so it seemed, the connection was
made which was both a resolution and an awakening.
It marked the beginning of a relationship that has
developed over the past 10 years and touches kindly
on the lives of our respective families. I am now the
proud 'owner' of three half-brothers. My natural
mother, Vee, has three additional grandchildren. And
my husband feels uniquely favoured with two
mothers-in-law!

I have learned a lot - about my emotional response to change, about nature and nurture, about the unconditional love of my parents, and about loss, prejudice and reconciliation.

Transitions

Consider the transitions in your own life. Some of these will have been welcomed - a new job perhaps, moving house, getting married or becoming a parent. Others will have been coloured with fear or anxiety, such as separation or divorce. Some will have been planned, while others will have occurred out of the blue. Here are a few more examples:

- beginning / ending of a relationship
- the death of someone close
- illness or injury
- promotion / redundancy
- inheriting money
- being 'betrayed'

Personal Responses

Every major transition event we experience involves loss - a shedding of the old skin, of the old self, of old ways of doing things. The process by which we come to terms with this can be divided into seven stages, illustrated here and popularly referred to as the *Transition Curve.** This way of examining our emotional response to change is particularly useful in relation to bereavement and loss.

* *Adapted from Hopson, Scally & Stafford - Transitions - The Challenge Of Change, Management Books 2000, 1993.*

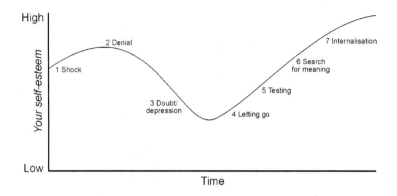

The vertical axis refers to our level of self-esteem; the horizontal axis, the time it takes for us to complete the transition. The scale and depth of the curve can vary enormously. Moving to a new house is a transition event, as is the death of a loved one. While we may experience the same *stages* of response, bereavement is likely to arouse a much greater depth of emotion and distress. It's like being on a roller-coaster, but you've no idea how long the ride is or how to work the brakes.

Here is a brief outline of each stage:

1   *Shock:* You feel overwhelmed. *I don't believe it.*

2   *Denial:* You try to make the change less than it is. *This   isn't really happening to me.*

3   *Doubt / depression:* Reality kicks in - a dark, difficult time, particularly in bereavement. *I can't do this.*

4   *Letting go:* You begin to accept the new situation. *I guess this is it.*

5   *Testing:* You test out ways of dealing with the new situation. *Perhaps I can try this . . .*

6 *Search for meaning:* You decide what actions are helpful. *This could work.*

7 *Internalisation:* You incorporate the transition into your life. *This is my way forward.*

Points to consider

Understanding how you respond to change and trauma puts you in a stronger position to help yourself and others. But remember the following:

- Each of us moves through the stages in our own time and way.

- We can get stuck and require support to move forward.

- We can fall back. Eg I remember receiving a sympathy letter from a friend months after I had a miscarriage, with the result that I slipped back into grief.

- The point of acceptance, or letting go, is a crucial stage in moving on.

- We may go through several changes at once, so the ride is more stressful.

- One change can create another in a domino effect. Eg a change of job can mean a different home and lifestyle. If family are involved, the scale of the change increases.

- You can apply the Transition Curve to the developmental changes we experience in our personal life cycle, as outlined next, but it's more relevant to life events.

You may never be confronted by the type of trauma which tears your life apart and rips everything you value away from you. But individuals *can* survive and grow from the most horrendous circumstances, because of the pulse inside us to move away from pain. The crucial element is how we support ourselves through the process.

Just Passing Through

In addition to *events*, we meet change in the ages and stages of our development. Age can seem so arbitrary. My chronological age is 42, but inside I feel about 25, outside I kid myself I look 35 (by candlelight) and sometimes I behave like a 12-year-old. Ask my children who builds the biggest snowmen in our family!

Judging from the media preoccupation with youth, you could be forgiven for thinking that there are no interesting life stages after 21. But Gail Sheehy's insightful mapping of life after youth explains some of the crises, or turning points, we experience in our later years and which, she says, are *predictable* and triggered not by external events, but by our internal life systems. The following is a brief outline of the stages she describes in *Passages - Predictable Crises of Adult Life* and *Pathfinders* (both Bantam 1997), to which interested readers are encouraged to refer.

Pulling up roots (18-22), marked by our search for independence and autonomy.

The Trying Twenties (23-27), characterised by attempts to establish ourselves in the adult world.

Catch-30 (28-33), when we may feel the first disappointments about choices we have made, which encourage us to 'make, break or deepen life commitments.' Sheehy describes the early-thirties stage (33-35), as Rooting and Extending, referring to our need to put down 'roots and shoots' in terms of home-making and career building.

Deadline Decade (35 - 45), which often includes the confusion and turmoil of midlife crisis in a major confrontation of the gap between where we aspired to be and where we actually are. We can be brought face to face with our own mortality and the reality of time passing.

The Comeback Decade (46-55), characterised by shifting perceptions as new roles and concerns come to the fore in preparation for the passage to middle age, which can be a time of stability, revitalisation or staleness.

The Freestyle Fifties, marked for those who have come through the 'dangerous' years leading up to their fifties in a positive manner, by a greater sense of happiness and acceptance.

The Selective Sixties, during which those of us who continue to be highly involved in the world around us often become more selective about what is important, and choose how full or active we want our life to be.

The Thoughtful Seventies, which can vary considerably according to how wide we make our world and the ways in which we are able to exert independence.

The *Proud-to-be-Eighties*, which may be marked by a continued interest in life, but can also involve a pre-occupation with oneself and one's illnesses and deficits. Those people who can still give of themselves to others will feel more positive than those who have become totally dependent.

You may find it helpful to consider how Maslow's Hierarchy of Needs (Chapter 1) might apply to us at different stages and ages of our lives. Other factors which influence our passages through the years will be our personal health, wealth and other physical, mental and emotional resources, as well as life experiences.

Pain And Gain

The ability to let go of old behaviours and attitudes is a precious skill. But it's easier said than done, especially when the past has been a friend. A colleague of mine even refers to her depression this way, although she is debilitated by it and dreams of a life without her dark skies. How difficult it must be to go forward, friendless.

Think about the most valuable things you have learned in your life. When did you learn them? Chances are that it was in times of particular challenge and difficulty, when you felt exposed and vulnerable and needed to rely on your own inner strength. When you meet an unwelcome change, you can do one of three things: deny it, resent it, or accept it and try and gain something from the experience. This last option was the one chosen by my friend Karen as outlined here . . .

On Hurt And Healing

Karen Brown, a physiotherapist, has lived the last three years at soap-opera pace. She and her family had moved to Scotland from Nottinghamshire and were just getting established, when, at the age of 41 and with two growing sons, she found out she was pregnant. Shock, disbelief and bleakness descended . . .

'As the mist cleared, I was able to see the way forward and went ahead with the pregnancy. I decided to have amniocentesis which added to the stress of the experience. It was at this time that I acquired a support network of friends and colleagues, which was to be crucially important over the next two years. The pregnancy proceeded to a happy conclusion with the birth of my third son, who is very special to me. I really thought we'd got through the storm.

'Three months later, I became ill and I was diagnosed with an acute over-active thyroid. I was encouraged to consider surgery and I duly went into hospital to have my thyroid removed, in what was to be a four-day stay for a fairly routine procedure.

Countdown to meltdown

'I emerged nine days later from an experience which virtually decimated my inner being. The operation itself went smoothly. It was only when complications set in, that both medical and nursing systems failed me. They failed me in their procedures, their management, their care and most importantly, their lack of humanity. Every time I thought things couldn't get worse they did. When I was finally discharged, I returned home physically drained and emotionally punch-drunk.

'To come so close to meltdown is breathtaking. Gradually I have made slow progress, but it has not been steady or smooth. A situation like this throws everything in your life into perspective. Nothing again will feel quite so scary or daunting. This is a process that seems to follow its own course. So I have gone along with it and am now up for total re-growth, regeneration and re-direction. Let's not stop at half a job!'

Action Points

* **Lifelines** - Compile a lifeline and mark the key transition events in your past, as in the example. Some people prefer to draw a wavy line, representing the peaks and troughs of their experiences.

Worked example:

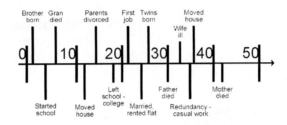

If this exercise creates anxiety, a useful option is to draw your future lifeline and mark the changes you *plan* to make.

- **Be kind to yourself** - There is no ideal response to change - simply your own. Don't punish yourself for being human. Find opportunities to express strong feelings, particularly painful ones, in ways that help you.
- **Build up areas of stability** - This will give you a stronger buffer against change.
  Elements that provide stability are:
  - a well-rounded lifestyle, with varied interests
  - fulfilling relationships
  - a network of people who will support you
  - a view of life which can ask *Why not me?* rather than *Why me?*
- **The time of your life** - Is this a period for you of challenge and change, or relative stability? What does that mean in terms of how you look after yourself? Consider too, how the *time* of the year / month / week / day affects you, so that you invest your energy wisely.
- **The best is yet to come** - Whatever age you are, ask yourself what you'd like to do when you grow up!

Summing Up . . .

The one constant in life is change. It can happen *to* us
or *from* us, but either way, it's all around us. This
chapter has explored three aspects: life events, ages
and stages, and personal responses.

Some transitions are planned - a new home, getting
married etc. But others simply occur - a chance
encounter, an accident, a sudden illness perhaps. In
the blink of an eye, lives can be enriched or torn apart;
we all walk that line. As we travel through the passages
of our adult life, there are also internally-driven
challenges and transitions to be tackled.

Whatever our personal experience of change, our
response tends to move through particular stages,
including denial and doubt, before we finally
internalise the transition and move on. Pain and gain
often go together. Many of our most valuable insights
about ourselves and others derive from our most
challenging times.

As my granny used to say: 'Whatever doesn't kill you
will make you stronger!'

Chapter 8

Meeting Stress

*Mental distress is doing the same thing over
and over again and expecting different results.*

- Worried lives
- Encounters with fear
- An occupational hazard
- From distress to de-stress
- Breaking the habit
- Action Points
- Summing up . . .

Worried Lives

We lead worried lives. We worry about what we look like, what we eat, whether we do the right thing, work in the right job, bring up our kids the right way. We worry about things that have happened, things we want to happen and things we fear might happen.

No wonder we feel stressed!

The long-term accumulation of these day-to-day worries can be as stressful as coping with major change. Anxiety erodes our confidence and distorts our thinking. Our worries and fears create stress and the more stressed we feel, the less able we are to deal with the hurdles and challenges we face. This feeds our fear that we won't be able to cope.

Stress, in fact, is simply a stimulus or demand made on our mental or physical energy. A manageable amount of stress is good for us because it makes us feel alive and alert, eg preparing for a new job or playing sports.

The problem occurs when stress becomes unmanageable, as when work or personal circumstances create relentless worry and tension, or when the amount of challenge we're dealing with gets out of hand. When the demands made on us exceed our ability to cope, stress kicks in. It's a delicate balance that can be maintained or upset by the way we act on our environment and our environment acts on us.

We also need to remember that something that is stressful for one person is not necessarily so for another. I know a woman, for example, who enjoys throwing herself off cliffs on the end of a bungee rope. But it's not *my* idea of fun. Her *stimulating challenge* is my *stress nightmare*. As we explored too, in the last chapter, many life events and changes - even ones we welcome - generate fear and anxiety and are therefore stressful.

Fight or flight

Our physiological response to positive and negative stress is the same - the adrenalin rush associated with fight or flight - nature's method of self-defence. This energises us to confront the 'enemy' or run, as our prehistoric ancestors were wont to do when faced with marauding hordes of wild pigs!

These natural defences are often suppressed, because we don't express our pent-up energy. Marauding pigs are thin on the ground and we tend not to fight the boss, physically at least, or flee the office. So the stress turns inwards . . .

Effects

The physical effects are well-known - headaches, digestive upsets, chest pain, dizziness, skin rashes, constipation or diarrhoea, and a tendency to illness and infection. But what about the emotional toll? The following responses are common:

- loss of self-esteem
- inability to concentrate
- loss of power / control
- irritable
- fearful
- victimised
- over-sensitive
- isolated

And causes?

Any area of life can become stressful. Identifying a cause is part of the solution, but many people find their distress defies easy definition. If this is the case for you, consider your emotional responses instead and identify any common threads. In the list above, the main theme seems to be *loss*.

What losses do *you* most fear? Health, strength, youth, looks, self-esteem, confidence, dignity, employment, status, money, relationships, possessions, home? How would you cope if any (or all) of these things were taken away?

If you recall Maslow's Hierarchy of Needs (Chapter 1), he argues that satisfying our basic needs for survival and safety is our priority. It follows that any threat to these needs brings us face-to-face with our ultimate fears. Once we have moved up to the 'higher order' needs - to belong, to achieve, and to be fulfilled - the loss of these will also threaten our identity. Personal wealth, access to health, education and transport, and the amount of personal freedom and security we possess, will also influence what we feel we *should have*, *want* and *need*. The more we have, the more we fear to lose.

Encounters With Fear

Facing our fears is the theme of Susan Jeffers' book *Feel The Fear And Do It Anyway* (Arrow 1991), in which she challenges us to turn fear and indecision into confidence and action. At the bottom of every one of our fears, she explains, is the fear that we cannot handle whatever life brings us. The way forward is to develop trust in our ability to handle whatever comes our way.

Christine Howden, a counsellor and groupworker specialising in stress management, lives *with* fear but not *in* fear. This is her story . . .

'MS is a disease which takes control . . . A series of radio appeals by the Multiple Sclerosis Society presented gloomy scenarios - people with MS unable to cook a meal without burning themselves, unable to play football with their kids, unable even to contemplate going on holiday. People out of control.

'The appeals attempted to trade on fear. And they contained a grain of truth. Fear is part of the human condition and MS brings this into focus. On my journey since 1987 with MS beside me, like an awkward relative who won't go away, I have met fear and stress in particular ways - my own and others'.

'Amidst the pain and confusion when I was diagnosed, was the conviction *I have brought this on myself.* Somehow I'd got it wrong in this business of living. I recognise now that I was protecting myself from something even more unbearable and fearful - from feeling helpless . . .

Appreciating the moment

'I had one encounter with a healer who announced cheerfully, 'You're *choosing* to have MS.' I disagree. I don't believe I have any choice about *having* MS. However I have a great deal of choice about how I *live with* MS. With the support of my therapist, I have learned to acknowledge my human vulnerability, to recognise that I am mortal and in many ways have little control over the future. Empowerment for me now includes embracing my helplessness.

'MS changes things - my relationship with others and my relationship with my body. My ability to walk, my balance, vision and energy can change dramatically, not just from day to day but from hour to hour. But MS won't take control of my life. I am more at peace, more appreciative of the present moment and life's abundance - the home near the sea I share with my husband, our garden, our wonderful cats, watching the moon and stars . . . Life isn't worse now - it's different.'

If I need your help, then I will ask. I know that you will give with all your heart. In the meantime, if you love me, let me struggle.

An Occupational Hazard

If you are in employment - paid or unpaid - it may not come as a surprise to hear that stress at work is considered to be one of the most serious occupational health issues of our time. It accounts for 100 million working days lost annually in the UK. It causes high staff turnover, reduces productivity and increases the risk of accidents. It also de-motivates and devalues individuals. One manager I knew, whose organisation was undergoing fundamental change, became so damaged by stress that he left his job following extended sick leave. If stress at work is an issue for you and your colleagues, you may find it useful to analyse why it's occurring and what you can do about it or influence others to do.

Just as personal stress results from an imbalance between the demands placed on us and our capacity to meet them, organisational stress can be created or exacerbated by an imbalance between market demands and organisational capability.

Stress in a cold climate

These demands, which often call on staff to work smarter and harder, can stretch even effective organisations to breaking point. And for individuals whose jobs have in-built stress, such as health and social workers, police and prison officers, the pressures can become intolerable.

When I delivered 'culture change' workshops to prison officers - whose involvement was crucial to the strategic development of their own prisons - many of them were so stressed by multiple demands on their time and energy, they could only perceive change negatively: less staff and more work.

Employers cannot prevent stress caused by a general lack of job security, but they can tackle other common causes. Do you recognise any of these in your workplace?

- bad communication
- 'them and us' culture
- dictatorial management
- bullying
- poor job design / work organisation
- lack of employee participation in decision-making

Grasping the nettle

Organisations which recognise and attempt to tackle the problem of stress at work may do so in different ways and at different levels. A useful start is a stress audit, to identify the nature of the problem, commonly carried out through questionnaires and focused discussion. It also provides baseline information for subsequent evaluation. Stress management actions, or interventions, are usually carried out on three levels: the *corporate*, or organisational level; the working group, or *team* level; and the *individual* level. These may involve:

Corporate level
- managers walking the job
- restructuring teams
- redesigning jobs / tasks
- flexible working
- 'better communication' initiatives
- more consultation

Team level
- team development training
- decision-making devolved to team level
- the team becoming responsible for whole processes
- co-operative working between and within teams

Individual level
- emphasis on training eg leadership, assertiveness, stress / time management
- personal development / career planning
- personal encouragement / support within team
- job transfers / secondments

If you are under stress at work, consider if any of these actions at the individual level might help. And raise the issue with colleagues, union representatives and managers so that it becomes something that is openly discussed. Organisations which acknowledge and address the problem bring some credibility to that over-used but under-practised phrase: *People are our most important asset.*

From Distress To De-stress

If there was a sure-fire way of moving from distress to de-stress, someone would have found it and made a million by sharing it with the rest of us. We would live in a Utopian world of peace, love and harmony. And pigs would fly.

Perhaps the realistic way forward lies somewhere between learning to manage ourselves better and adopting a perspective that enables us to engage in life less fearfully. That and 101 handy hints for reducing hassle!

How are you doing just now?

You will already have found ways of coping with stress in your life. Jot down your coping mechanisms alongside the list on the left, which was compiled by participants on a stress management course. Draw your own comparisons.

Theirs	Yours
Take tranquillisers, sleeping pills	
Watch TV	
Cry, scream, shout	
Go to bed	
Take time off work	
Pamper myself with treats	
Withdraw	
Rely on others for support	
Smoke / eat / drink too much	

These activities tend to fall into one or more of the categories which I have outlined in the following boxes. You could note your own examples in the appropriate box to help you identify whether you would like to develop alternative / further ways of coping in any of the categories. Activities which fall into the Action box are particularly important because they can *prevent* stress. Note that this category includes saying *no*!

Action	Self-expression
eg say no, delegate	eg cry, scream, shout
Diversion	Self-care
eg watch TV	eg warm bath, rest

Breaking The Habit

As the stress of Jonathan's lifestyle increased, coping mechanisms weren't enough. So he changed his habits . . . and his solution has embraced wholeness and well-ness as a life purpose and career.

An artist and craftsman, Jonathan worked as a potter in Cumbria for 15 years, building a flourishing business. But in the process, he severely injured his back. 'It was outcome at the expense of procedure,' he explains, as he recounts the painful memory of cortisone injections and osteopathy on his spine.

This led him to explore the Alexander Technique - a way of increasing awareness of poise and movement, and releasing limiting habits - and he is now a practitioner. 'It started to wake me up to my body processes, to my patterned ritual of behaviour and to the level of dysfunction in my life. I had to break the habit . . . '

Further training in Transactional Analysis (see Parents, Adults and Children, Chapter 10) built on his understanding and experience of the Alexander Principle and underlined the importance of conscious awareness and choice about how we think and behave, particularly in times of stress. He has incorporated this into his own work as a trainer and adviser in personal development initiatives.

'We can change our responses to the feelings we have. We can change what we believe about ourselves and we can change how we behave. This level of consciousness will bring about some capacity to identify what we are doing, to manage it and to take responsibility for it.'

It is particularly important for men, he feels, to tune into themselves on a deeper level and explore aspects of their distress rather than deny or avoid it. 'Our work culture, particularly, has lost meaning for a lot of men. We all need to touch our sense of loss before moving on. It is a powerful and painful experience, but it enables us to break the habits of a lifetime and release our true potential.'

Action Points

*   **Source your stress** - Think about the main sources of stress for you just now, using this list as a prompt:
    *   personal relationships
    *   home / work conflict
    *   work issues
    *   personal circumstances - health, money, housing etc
    *   life events
    *   bad memories
    *   the way you spend your time
    *   your age or stage of life

    Choose one source of stress to deal with *now*, either through new ways of coping or by acting to prevent the problem. The following exercises may help:

- **Just the boss' fault?** - What point on this scale describes your commitment to:
  (a) your job (b) your working group and (c) your
    organisation?

Very low	Low	Average	High	Very high

  What stresses are built into your job because of
  (a) your role? (b) the way individuals and groups work together and (c) the way the organisation does things?

- **No time for a crisis** - Beat the clock by using your time more effectively. Differentiate between what is *urgent* and *important*. Important activities meet your priorities and help you reach your goals. Urgent activities come with deadlines attached, but they may or may not be important . . .

- **Fighting back** - Look back over the list of coping mechanisms in From Distress To De-stress and think about some of the pros and cons of each method for you, including the ones you have not used before and any others you have added.

  - Which are the most effective ways of coping for you?
  - Why do they work for you?
  - Can you understand why people have identified other methods?
  - Are there any ways of coping you haven't used, but might find helpful to try?
  - Are there any methods you currently use which you'd like to stop using?
  - What actions might you take to stop stress building up in the first place?

- **So what would *you* do *without* your worries?** Answers on a postcard please . . . or perhaps something bigger?

Summing Up . . .

Life is a source of stress. But this doesn't mean that stress has to become a way of life. This chapter has looked at how we might define and manage stress both at home and at work.

Identifying the effects is often easier than defining the causes. Exploring our responses to stress can be helpful in identifying the source of the problem. Much of our anxiety is often around the fears we have about loss and our inability to cope with what comes our way.

We can choose to live with fear rather than in fear, and retain our confidence and control. This is the view shared by counsellor and groupworker Christine Howden, who exercises the right to choose her way of life, as she journeys with multiple sclerosis 'like an awkward relative who won't go away.'

There is no magic formula for moving from distress to de-stress, but we can develop our own coping mechanisms. We can also break out of our stress-inducing habits of a lifetime and go for wholesale change.

For worriers in general, and young worriers in particular, the *Huge Bag of Worries*, produced by the charity Children 1st,*contains the following advice:

'If you have a worry, don't keep it to yourself. It will just get BIGGER and BIGGER. Share it with someone else.'

* see the Further Reading section in the Help List

Note - If you find yourself in a constant state of fear and anxiety, you may benefit from specialised support available through health services, community projects and self-help groups. Contact your GP and refer to the Help List at the back of this book.

Part Four

Know The Skills You Need

Chapter 9

Developing Assertiveness

*Eavesdroppings . . . overheard on London Underground,
one man to another:*

*'Don't let your wife near one of those assertiveness training
classes. It's been downhill all the way since mine went. And
it's playing havoc with my darts!'*

- Hello, I'm over here!
- Man or mouse?
- A walk on the wild side
- In at the deep end
- Winning ways
- Action Points
- Summing up . . .

Hello, I'm Over Here!

I was walking down a city street recently, when I
passed a man standing in the middle of the pavement,
shouting one phrase continually and passionately at
passers-by: 'Why won't people listen to each other's
problems?' People may have heard him, but they
pretended he wasn't there, which is probably the
answer to his question.

In a world full to bursting with information and
communication, relating to each other is still a tricky
business. And that's assuming someone pays you some

attention. Being invisible is a sign of our times and is an issue which regularly emerges at assertiveness classes. Here are some typical comments:

- *I wish I weren't such a wimp.*
- *I can deal with my boss, but I'm afraid to tackle my partner.*
- *My daughter's getting bullied at school. How can I help her stand up for herself?*

Developing assertiveness enables you to be *less* of a wimp, *more able* to tackle your partner, to *help* your children stand up for themselves and, most importantly, to be *seen* and to be *heeded* as well as heard.

But before you storm the barricades, assertiveness *isn't* about getting your own way at any price. Neither is it about playing games. I remember one female client cooing softly, 'I don't actually *need* assertiveness, Linda. I wind men around my little finger with charm and sex appeal.' On a spectrum of assertiveness between *marshmallow* and *Arnold Schwarzenegger,* I gave that comment a score of *candy floss.* Time then, to shed some light on the subject?

Let's have a bit of respect

Assertiveness is about respect - for yourself and others. This involves rights *and* responsibilities, like any other exercise of personal power. So it's also about:

- standing up for your rights without violating other people's rights
- being open and honest
- listening to others
- expressing yourself clearly, with care and consideration
- working constructively with tension, problems or disagreement

Seen in this light, assertiveness is a way of behaving which would benefit everyone, including the darts player I quoted at the beginning of the chapter!

Bill of Rights

You, me, the butcher, the baker and the candlestick maker, we're all assertive, sometimes.

We tend to be naturally assertive in situations where we feel comfortable and confident.

Developing assertiveness, therefore, is about extending your natural ability into what are difficult or unnatural situations for you. In order to do this, you need a conscious awareness of your rights. Here is the list I use on assertiveness courses:

- I have the right to be treated with respect
- I have the right to be treated as an individual and an equal
- I have the right to express my feelings and opinions
- I have the right to be listened to
- I have the right to choose the life I lead
- I have the right to ask for my needs to be met
- I have the right to make mistakes
- I have the right to make my own decisions
- I have the right to decline responsibility for other people's problems
- I have the right *not* to be assertive!

Man Or Mouse?

We've all been there, whether the situation is in a doctor's surgery, a shop, in the street, at work or at home. You fail miserably to assert yourself and feel grossly inadequate, or you lose control and blow your top.

These situations happen to us and around us. I remember seeing two mothers, both gentle-natured souls, completely lose control while waiting for their offspring at the school gates. They started arguing about their children and all of a sudden, hell had no fury like wee Johnny's mother scorned. I thought the school lollipop man was going to have to prise them apart. Fortunately the bell went.

When we meet a difficult situation, there are basically four types of response:

- aggressive
- passive
- manipulative
- assertive

The aggressive response is linked with fight, the passive response, with flight. The manipulative response is indirectly aggressive, using emotional blackmail to extract the desired outcome. Beware of condemning these non-assertive behaviours too harshly - they all have a use. What is important is your ability to choose the appropriate behaviour for you.

Here's a brief summary of the four behaviours:

Behaviour	Characteristics	Advantages	Disadvantages
Aggressive	Forceful, often hurtful	High impact	Others get hurt

Eg: (teacher to pupils) You lot are so stupid! Why did I get a class like you?

Passive	Timid, self-deprecating	Stay 'safe'	Can stay a victim

Eg: I'm sorry you trod on my foot.

Manipulative	Controlling games	Can win the game	Builds resentment

Eg: (mother to daughter) If you insist on inviting your cousin to the wedding, your father might be unable to attend.

Assertive	Positive acceptance	Builds confidence & respect	Others don't always welcome such candour!

Eg: I appreciate your concerns about my proposal. Can we discuss them?

A Walk On The Wild Side

Julia is a woman who recognises the right to be herself. But the journey to this point of acceptance has been a walk on the wild side.

Until her early 30s, life had gone fairly smoothly. Running a home and holding down a full-time job, whilst supporting her husband and young son, didn't leave much time for herself. And making ends meet was a close-run thing. But all in all, it was OK.

The crises hit home like the steady drip of a leaking tap. Following a traumatic pregnancy, her second son was born, happily, with the minimum of distress. But he required brain surgery. Within weeks of the birth, she found that her job with an advertising agency was no longer open to her after maternity leave. On top of this, her marriage failed.

Fighting back

'Re-building my life in these circumstances required a level of assertiveness that was out of character,' she says. 'But I had to fight back. I had two children, and as the breadwinner, I literally couldn't afford to be a victim.'

And fight back, she did. Between hospital appointments with her infant son, and despite the distress in her personal life, she took the advertising agency to an Industrial Tribunal for unfair dismissal under the Sex Discrimination Act - and won £25,000 compensation.

Her son's brain operation, at the age of four months, went smoothly and finding another job began to restore her confidence. Life as a single parent has brought compensations . . .

'When your life goes pear-shaped, you have to find your own way of doing things. I had lived life for so long on other people's terms, I didn't know what my terms were. I had set great store by having a husband, children, a job, home and salary. I did a major re-think. My focus now is managing myself and caring for the children.

'Assertiveness for me is about valuing myself and expressing my feelings, whether I am negotiating with my boss over marketing plans, or with my ex-husband over access arrangements. I have surprised myself by my own capacity to manage difficult situations. I believe that I have the right to take up space in this world and be me.'

In At The Deep End

Let's look at some situations which test your ability to behave assertively. How easy or difficult do you find the following? Answer according to the degree of difficulty experienced, on a scale of 1 to 5, where 1 = very easy and 5 = very difficult.

Situation   Score (1 - 5)

1   Saying *no* to requests from friends /
     family / boss
2   Coping with others' outbursts of
     emotion
3   Giving someone bad news
4   Resolving a serious personal
     disagreement
5   Public speaking
6   Admitting you have made a mistake
7   Dealing with bullying / sexual
     harassment
8   Receiving criticism (justified and
     unjustified)
9   Confronting a loved one
10   Helping others become more
     assertive

Do your responses indicate any common factors amongst your most difficult situations?

What are the factors that help or hinder you in behaving assertively? What can you do about them?

You may like to draw up your Top 10 situations - from the mildly irritating to the most daunting - in which you would like to behave more assertively, using the list here as a prompt. The idea is that you practise being more assertive in minor situations, so that you become more able to tackle the major ones when you have honed your skills. Today, your mother-in-law; tomorrow, the world!

Be patient with yourself. There is a world of difference between the theory and the practice of assertiveness. This is why assertiveness trainers love role play. Practice makes perfect.

Winning Ways

Assertive communication often involves co-operation and compromise. If you think of any negotiation between individuals or groups, the outcome falls into one of four basic categories, which relates to the *I'm OK You're OK* model (Thomas Harris) introduced in Chapter 4:

I win, You lose = I'm OK, You're not OK
Aggressive / Manipulative

I lose, You win = I'm not OK, You're OK
Passive

I lose, You lose = I'm not OK, You're not OK
Aggressive / Manipulative

I win, You win = I'm OK, You're OK
Assertive

If you believe you can only win at someone else's expense, or that any discussion is pointless, your attitude is likely to be aggressive or manipulative. If you think you have to back down in order to resolve a problem, your attitude is likely to be passive. But if you believe that each person's needs can be considered - even if not satisfied - you will behave assertively in search of mutual agreement and benefit.

Working with conflict may well feature in your Top 10 difficult situations. So here are some ideas to consider, whether initiating a discussion or responding:

- Listen to understand the other person. Ask questions if you need clarification.

- Show you understand their point of view. Repeat it back to them eg *As I understand it, what you are saying is* . . . You don't have to agree with it.

- Own and express your own feelings: *I feel* _____ *when you* _____'

- Say what you'd like to happen.

- Keep calm.

- Seek joint agreement and solutions.

None of this will guarantee a *win-win* result, but you will feel more confident about the encounter and emerge with your self-respect intact rather than in tatters.

Action Points

- **Practise saying no** - Identify situations in which you can't say no and ask yourself why. Are you unclear, unsure, or easily manipulated? Practise saying no in front of a mirror to find out what you look like. If your body language doesn't match your verbal message, you may sabotage yourself. The key is to be direct and avoid excessive apology or justification. Say no in your reply and speak as though you were telling someone the time: *No, I'm afraid that won't be possible . . . (It's half-past three).*

- **Develop strategies for dealing with difficult people -**

  These include:

  Broken Record - persist in putting your point across like a record stuck in its groove, eg on returning faulty goods . . . *I would prefer a refund thank you,* repeated until you get it!

  Negative Assertion - acknowledge your faults and mistakes, but don't grovel, eg *Yes, I agree it was wrong of me to do that, but I was trying to help.*

  Negative Enquiry - ask for more information about a problem or error, eg *I'm aware I miscalculated that payment. Are there any other mistakes I should know about?*

- **Be assertive for a change** - Consider specific situations or relationships you could improve by changing your behaviour. Apply the *stop / start* method, by identifying three things to stop doing and three things to start doing:

  I will stop

  eg I will stop apologising so much

  _____

  _____

  _____

  I will start

  eg I will start showing my son how much I appreciate his support

  _____

  _____

  _____

- **Compile your own Bill of Rights** - Base it on the list in this chapter or start from scratch. Begin the statements in the same way, ie I have the right to . . . Encourage your children to do their list. Mine came up with:

  - I have the right to stand up for myself and others
  - I have the right to say no
  - I have the right to be respected and not to be bullied
  - I have the right to ask for help and information

- **Speak out** - If you are good at speaking up, learn to speak out. Strengthen the voice of individuals or groups in your community who are not being listened to. Make them visible.

Summing Up . . .

This chapter has defined assertiveness in terms of respect for self and others. It is not about aggression, with which it is often confused.

You are already assertive in situations where you feel confident and comfortable.

Developing assertiveness is about handling difficult situations - whether that be getting attention, or resolving a conflict - by expressing yourself with care and consideration, rather than automatically being submissive, or losing control.

Whatever assertiveness tools and techniques you apply, they will be effective only when used with integrity. If you are conscious of your rights *and* responsibilities, then winning at someone else's expense will be less important than striving for mutual benefit - win-win. This doesn't guarantee that everyone will share your point of view, but you will emerge from close encounters of the challenging kind with your self-respect intact.

Like Julia, who recounts her 'walk on the wild side,' you have the right to take up space in this world and be yourself.

Chapter 10

Developing Communication

When people not used to speaking out are heard by people not used to listening, then real changes can be made.
John O'Brien

- Straight talking - there's nothing like it!
- Positive impressions
- Listen to me!
- Parents, adults and children
- On your wavelength
- Action Points
- Summing up . . .

One of life's little mysteries for my family is how I can be on the 'phone for hours to a friend and still find plenty to talk about when I see them later the same day! My response is predictable (thanks to BT): 'It's good to talk.'

Every day, we share ideas, information and feelings with friends, family, colleagues and managers, partners and strangers. We do it even when we're not speaking - in the blink of an eye, a shrug or a hug. But that doesn't mean we always get our message across or that we 'hear' the messages other people send us.

We have seen how assertiveness is crucial to effective communication. Other issues we have explored are also relevant:

- *Your self-esteem* - if you are confident to communicate, you'll be more competent.

- *Your motivation* - if you *want* to communicate you will be more effective.

- *The way you talk to yourself* - putting yourself down can undermine your message.

- *Your self-awareness* - if you know yourself well, you will be better able to control the way you give and receive information.

- *Your relationship* - if you have (or can adopt) a positive attitude to the other person, communication will be more straightforward.

Straight Talking - There's Nothing Like It!

There's nothing like straight talking. But you can almost see the thought bubbles in some people's heads contradicting the words tripping out their mouths.

Maggie and Pam meet in the supermarket . . .

Maggie *says*: 'Hi Pam. How are you? You *do* look well. How are those boys of yours?'

Maggie *thinks*: My God, you look 10 years older and your roots are showing. I bet your kids are giving you hell.

Pam *says*: 'We're all fine thanks. Must get together for coffee soon.'

Pam *thinks*: Hell! Just my luck to bump into you. No we're not fine. My life's falling apart. Coffee with you? No way!

Communication or shadow boxing?

Mike meets Sian for his performance review:

The main ingredient

The main ingredient of effective communication - missing from these dialogues - is *positive regard*. You would not speak (or think) this way with a close friend. With someone you respect and trust, you tend to say what you mean and mean what you say.

There are advantages to this:

- it builds understanding
- it makes you feel good
- it encourages openness
- it helps you get to the heart of the matter

Being straightforward in our communication with each other also saves time!

Positive Impressions

We can extend this positive approach to the way we present ourselves. We are judged by the impression we make, which research suggests is divided into:

- 55% appearance and body language
- 38% tone of voice
- 7% verbal content

If appearance and tone of voice are so powerful, make sure you are perceived the way you intend by communicating in a way which:

- is clear and appropriate
- shows your personality
- puts the other person at ease

Maintaining eye contact, smiling and listening all strengthen your ability to make others feel comfortable in your company, thereby encouraging a more open exchange.

Assuming confidence

You may not always *feel* confident, but *assuming* confidence can help you create a positive impression.

So what does confidence look and sound like?

- an upright posture
- relaxed and attentive
- good eye contact
- an even tone of voice

My first attempt at public speaking was before an audience of 50 managers. I was petrified. The only way to survive the lions' den was to pretend that I did this every day. So I slowed my speech, lowered my voice, and managed to look a few of them in the eye. It worked. I didn't get eaten and this experience taught me that assuming confidence helps build it.

Listen To Me!

We are taught to read and write. But listening - the most crucial skill in building and maintaining relationships - is largely taken for granted. How often do we really listen to another person, tune into them, enter their world, even on an everyday level? We can be so keen to judge, give advice, make suggestions and solve problems, that the listening, and the hearing, are lost.

Rob Warren knows how powerful listening can be, particularly in the context of supporting people. He is team leader of the Royal Edinburgh Hospital Patients' Council and was formerly the Director of the Citizens' Advocacy Alliance in London, the first such group to be set up in the UK.

'The whole art of listening is about being *present* to someone, not only hearing the words, but understanding the content of what is being said,' he says. 'There are so many ways a person can talk to you. It's not necessarily about words, it's about understanding *where that person is.'*

The process of listening, he explains, has to begin with an awareness of how we, as individuals, learn, hear and understand others. Only then can we use that awareness to build relationships.

Stepping into the silence

He tells the story of Phil, a man in his early 20s, who was unable to talk. Phil lived in a hospital for people with learning disabilities on the 'challenging behaviour' ward. He had no one in his life to whom he could relate and he was locked into a system in which others viewed him as beyond hope.

He was introduced, through a local advocacy organisation, to a woman who came from a different world - comfortable and privileged by comparison. To begin with, he couldn't be *with her* in any sense when she visited him. But she kept turning up anyway. Over a period of time, he started to trust her and she, through her tenacity, began to understand him.

As he gradually responded to her, so the staff changed their perception of him. The vicious circle turned into a virtuous one. He began to go out for days, then weekends, as his advocacy partner introduced him to her family and the wider circles of her own life. He lost the 'challenging behaviour' label and began to prepare for life outside hospital. He had been heard and valued as someone who was important, with something to say.

'With people who are devalued, ignored, left out, considered to be not fully-paid-up members of society,' says Rob, 'I think there's an onus on us to stand in their shoes, to walk that extra mile.'

Parents, Adults And Children

Aspects of our personality also affect the way we talk and listen. Do you let the child in you come out to play? My inner child pops out regularly - fun-loving minx that she is. But I have an inner parent and an inner adult too. Being a mum, I have an abundance of parental wisdom, eg 'If you don't wear your slippers, you'll get cold feet!' Meanwhile, my adult side hovers in the background, poised to do the *Telegraph* crossword!

The idea that we all have Parent, Adult and Child 'ego-states' is explained by Dr Eric Berne in the theory of Transactional Analysis contained within his book *Games People Play*, to which I have already referred (Chapter 4, stroke theory).

Who's who?

Our *Parent* replays messages we received from our own parents, which may reflect nurture and control. Our *Child* just wants to have fun, but can also be *childish,* complete with tantrums. And our *Adult* is our logical, rational side, keeping our Parent and Child in check. The mature person is, apparently, a balance of all three. The theory is that we communicate by means of *transactions,* each of us operating out of Parent, Adult or Child (PAC) modes according to the way we behave in different situations. This produces a possible nine combinations and numerous potential misunderstandings.

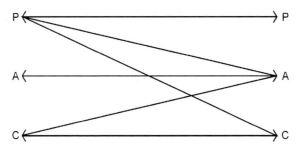

Let's see some combinations in practice . . . Louise is late for an evening meeting and has lost her handbag. She is childlike in her plea to flat mate Dave, who is relaxing after a hard day . . . 'I've lost my handbag. Can you help me?'

Here are three different replies from Dave:

1 (impatiently) 'Where did you put it last? You really *should* take more care.'

2 'Leave me alone! I'm watching TV.'

3 'It's on the dresser in the kitchen.'

No prizes for guessing which responses represent Parent, Child and Adult (they were in that order) and which Louise prefers.

Improving communication

If there is a balance of exchange, eg Adult - Adult (which you can equate with *I'm OK, You're OK*), it works fine. But if the lines get crossed, the communication becomes unsatisfactory. This doesn't mean that Adult-Adult is the only satisfactory exchange. The important thing is that they're *complementary*. If I am distressed and feeling childlike, I will value a nurturing 'parent' response from my partner - a hug, a cup of tea etc. But if I need to talk adult-to-adult about my concerns and my partner pats me on the head and tells me to worry, we will have crossed lines.

By becoming more aware of these aspects of our personality, we can perhaps change any unhelpful habits and get into balance.

On Your Wavelength

It's great when someone is 'on your wavelength,' but it may not be chemistry or coincidence. Rapport is created through active listening, which includes an ability to read non-verbal communication. Some people also 'click' because they share ways of perceiving the world around them and expressing themselves. An understanding of the idea of brain dominance and different sensory modes can be helpful here.

Brain dominance

The brain has right and left hemispheres which control different functions, and the theory is that we tend to have a dominant side. A typical left-brainer is said to be logical, analytical and organised, whilst a right-brainer is seen as being imaginative and creative.

Whilst we can play to our strengths, we may need to work harder at things which use the non-dominant side of our brain. If you are an intuitive right-brainer, you may have difficulty with practical tasks. I once failed to intuitively assemble a set of shelves! Equally, if you are a logical left-brainer, you may be thrown by complex interpersonal issues. Which are you?

Consider how you might enrich your communication, particularly within a group, by using fact and imagery, practical detail and the broader view, to appeal to right *and* left-brainers. Television adverts are a rich source of learning about making things memorable.

Sensory preferences

We may also have a preferred sensory mode. Although we have five senses, the three most common in communication are seeing, hearing and feeling. There may be an element of smelling and tasting, but usually after the 9pm watershed!

Think about some of the phrases you use:

- *I see what you mean.*
- *What's your point of view?*
  Are you someone who thinks visually?

- *That name rings a bell.*
- *I hear what you say.*
  Are you someone who thinks aurally?

- *I've got a feel for this.*
- *Are you comfortable with that?*
  Are you someone who thinks kinaesthetically, in terms of physical feelings?

The idea is that we can build rapport by identifying and matching other people's preferred sensory mode, encouraging them to feel we're on their wavelength. Then we can extend this matching process by consciously mirroring their body language and copying their pace of speech. Have you noticed how lovers unconsciously mirror each other?

Taking the idea a stage further, once you have established rapport, you can encourage the other person to adopt *your* body language or pace of speech, eg encouraging someone who is chattering excitedly to slow down by speaking slowly yourself. Building rapport can be particularly useful in diffusing tense situations. Next time you find yourself getting involved in a heated discussion, soften your voice to a whisper and see what happens. Whilst this is my pet technique for surviving the noise and chaos of *adolescent angst* in our household (characterised by cries of 'It's not fair!'), I have noticed that said adolescents prefer volume.

Action Points

- **See yourself as others see you** - How do other people perceive you as a communicator? Are you a talker or a listener? Ask for feedback. If you're feeling brave, ask if you have any unconscious habits, like twiddling your hair, stroking your nose, sniffing, mumbling etc!
- **Stand in someone else's shoes** - Make time to really listen to someone you don't normally have a lot of time for. Listen with your eyes as well as your ears. Practise this skill consciously and widely, until it becomes part of you.

- **Changing places** - Recall a 'difficult' conversation you have had and decide which part (Parent, Adult or Child) you and the other person each adopted. Would it have made a difference if either or both of you had changed parts? How might you handle a similar situation in the future?

- **Practise being precise** - We tend to use woolly words and phrases through habit or nervousness, when being specific will increase our chances of being understood. Add to my examples with your own.
    - Just at this moment in time — *now*
    - I'm not sure that I am going to be able to accede to your request — *no*
    - May I express my regret at the way in which this was handled — *I'm sorry for the mistake.*

_____

_____

_____

- **Repair communication errors** - We can all say the wrong thing innocently. If it happens *to* you, don't take it too personally and if you offend someone else, try to repair the mistake with honesty and humour. The best tip I have heard for stress prevention is *not to take things personally*!

- **Help with communication problems** - If you have difficulties with reading, writing or spelling, consider joining one of many adult learning projects operated by education services and local groups. See Help List - Learning Direct. Your local community education office will have details of projects available in your area. Many colleges also run Study Skills courses, creative writing workshops and discussion groups to encourage participants to become more confident communicators.

- **Walk your talk** - Let your actions reflect your words, not contradict them.

Summing Up . . .

For something we do every day of our lives, communicating is still hard work. This chapter has illustrated the value of self-knowledge and assertiveness in saying what we mean and meaning what we say; creating a positive impression, and, most importantly, listening to others to stand in their shoes and understand them.

Interpersonal communication can also be developed by addressing different aspects of our personality. The theory of Transactional Analysis, put forward by Dr Eric Berne, suggests that we have within us a Parent, Adult and Child which affects the way we behave. When two people meet in complementary modes, the communication is positive, but when lines get crossed, sparks can fly.

Feeling that we're 'on the same wavelength' as someone else is a joy, but our ability to connect can be developed. An awareness of the theory of brain dominance and different sensory modes can help identify common 'wavelengths' and build rapport in situations of conflict.

Misunderstandings will always occur, but you can repair communication errors with honesty and humour . . .

'What a *stink*,' pronounced my daughter as she caught a whiff of the manure being spread on the field outside our house.

'We've done a project about that,' piped up my son (circa Primary 2). 'Dinosaurs are extinct!'

Chapter 11

Developing Self-Care

To see a world in a grain of sand
And a heaven in a wild flower
Hold infinity in the palm of your hand
And eternity in an hour.
William Blake, Auguries of Innocence

* Self-care and pleasure
* Self-care and pain
* 'It's not what you call me . . .'
* Self-care and potential
* Action Points
* Summing up . . .

Caring for yourself is a process, not an end state. It's not a quick fix or a DIY make-over. On one level, the whole of this book is about self-care, because it's a celebration of your individuality and potential. But we are paying particular attention here to maintaining and developing your wholeness and well-being in order to end on a nurturing note. Sheer indulgence.

Self-Care And Pleasure

Why is it that if you ask people if they're happy, they usually need to stop and think about it? Then they'll probably define the word before they give you an answer. Is happiness really so elusive or is it a state of mind that simply doesn't fit with living in a divided society in a divided world?

Think of an occasion when you felt radiant with happiness, when you did indeed, in the words of Blake, 'hold infinity in the palm of your hand.' When it happens, it's unforgettable. We may not be able to turn it on at will, like a light switch, but perhaps we can make these occasions more likely and more common, by working on our capacity to experience pleasure.

Karen, whose story appears in Chapter 7, awards herself *pleasure points* on a regular basis. If this sounds like some kind of customer loyalty card, well maybe it is. She tries to set time out for herself on a regular basis, to have a game of golf perhaps, meet up with friends, or take a swim. She gives herself bonus points in times of stress. It may sound trivial, but this attitude has helped her through the most difficult time of her life.

Many people view pleasure as something that has to be earned through blood, sweat and tears. There is much to be said for working to achieve something, but not to the exclusion of those simpler pleasures that can be ours for the price and effort of becoming aware of what's in front of our nose.

Treat-time

What are the simple pleasures you most enjoy? If this exercise seems reminiscent of 'whiskers on kittens and warm woollen mittens,' well I like apple strudel too, and these are some of *my* favourite things:

- a walk in the country
- enjoying a meal with friends
- a visit to the cinema / theatre
- meeting friends for coffee / shopping
- a long hot bath
- sitting by a coal fire
- hot chocolate
- having a laugh with the family

Draw up your own list of *at least* a dozen treats. Include things you enjoy alone and those you enjoy in company; those which you can enjoy at any time and those which require planning; and treats which cost nothing alongside those which incur some expenditure. The longer your list, the better. Award yourself pleasure points regularly, with bonus points at times of challenge and change. Have some of them on special offer and give yourself three for the price of two!

Body-wise

Our physical image is shaped by age, gender, health and fitness, but regular exercise and good nutrition will make you look and feel better. My own definition of the main food groups used to be chocolate, cholesterol, additives and burnt crispy bits. But I've cut down on the cholesterol and the additives.

Here are a few more pointers to self-care:

- Get adequate sleep and exercise.
- Take a vitamin supplement if it's helpful.
- Learn about stress and act to reduce / alleviate it.

- Learn methods and techniques for relaxation. Know your personal tension areas. Explore complementary therapies such as aromatherapy, reflexology, yoga, massage, Alexander Technique etc for pleasure, health and well-being.

- Dress in a way that makes you feel comfortable.

- Nourish yourself through meditation, calm reflection or prayer - whatever is appropriate to your personal spiritual and religious beliefs.

- Find things or people that make you *smile*!

Self-Care And Pain

Life hurts. Love hurts. No one is immune from pain and distress. And there are some things that cannot be mended. All the treats and pleasure points in the world won't take away the pain of profound grief or loss. Self-care in the midst of the worst that life can throw at us becomes a different concept. The challenge of caring for oneself in such circumstances may be about how much support we are able to let others give us . . .

'I went to pieces when my 16-year-old son died,' says Nina. 'I didn't want to go on. I couldn't eat. I wore the same clothes for days, couldn't sleep, couldn't go out, couldn't even think much. I caught sight of myself in the mirror one morning. There was this old grey-looking woman. I didn't recognise myself. I had disappeared. So I 'phoned the Samaritans and I know now that this was a turning-point.'

There are no certain guidelines for moving forward, but the following ideas may be helpful:

- Self-care in a time of crisis is about keeping going.

- Talk to someone. It can be a lifeline.

- Take each day as it comes and one thing at a time.

- Keep eating, even if food tastes like cotton wool.

- Don't put on an act.

- Spend time with people who will support you.

- Express your feelings in a safe place.

- Ask questions.

- Go back to basics.

- Be loving to yourself.

On a cautionary note . . .

There is a growing army of professional helpers, therapists and counsellors. Whilst this source of support can be immensely valuable, there are risks and limitations. A friend who was encouraged by a counsellor to attend an anger management course was still recovering from the experience weeks later. While on the course, she felt coerced into talking about memories of abuse she had previously laid to rest. Other people have been distressed to be told that they are the cause of their own illness or disease. My advice is - go carefully. Keep control of whatever form of help you choose.

'It's Not What You Call Me . . . '

Heather Davidson's understanding of self-care has taken on a new dimension in the past three years, since she sustained a serious head injury, at the age of 23, which caused her life to turn full circle . . .

'In a matter of seconds, I was stripped of abilities I took for granted and faced the almost insurmountable task of rehabilitation. In times of blinding crisis, we are thrust a one-way ticket by the ugly hand of fate - destination unknown. Personally I was filled with terror at the thought of going it alone, but the solo journey makes for a concentrated traveller who in time, has lessons to learn and wisdom to bestow.

'Self-care for me encompasses a vast range of topics from nutrition to psychology. The emotions I feel on a daily basis are confusion, anger, self-pity, grief, disbelief, regret, fear, embarrassment, acceptance, achievement, perception and occasionally, overwhelming joy.

'It is often hard to listen to people talk passionately of careers, property, holidays, money and their battles through daily life. Do they understand the purity and innocence of the struggle against twisted circumstance? Part of self-care is the ability to come through this experience, learn by it and pass on wisdom in a gentle tone.'

Don't gaze back

To others grieving for the life they once lived, she offers: 'Don't gaze back. Concentrate on today. If you can't face the comparison between your past and your present, rest where you are and don't give it any thought for now. Avoid the temptation to assess the long road ahead.'

'Circumstance or disability need not belittle you, for spirit is monumental. Others may never feel your inner power or understand your calming peace, but they, in jealous ignorance, may attempt to twist your achievements with bitter words. Take to heart the old African proverb - 'It is not what you call me, but what I answer to.'

'You may be hurled to the ground, beaten and bruised, but by God, you *will* rise.'

Self-Care And Potential

Each of us is more than the sum of our parts. You have more potential for joy, health, growth, self-expression and achievement than you will ever realise. And your ability to live life more fully is your own. Taking care of your physical, spiritual and emotional well-being strengthens your inner resources to empower, enable and protect you.

Harmony and wholeness are valuable things to strive for and these involve a balance:

*   Between the roles in your life.

*   Between work and play; activity and rest; social contact and solitude; noise and quiet; engagement and withdrawal; stability and change.

*   Between mind, body and spirit.

*   In your relationships. If you build your entire life around one relationship, you are particularly vulnerable to its loss, or fear of loss.

*   Between giving of yourself and taking from others.

- Between striving for things you don't have and appreciating the things you do have.

- Between doing everything yourself and seeking support from others.

Build your own future

Finding your own balance will help you align your actions with your priorities and values and give you the courage and confidence *to be what you can be* and *do what you can do*. Let's remind ourselves of the impact that confidence has on what we do and feel. The responses have been suggested by a group of men and women who work as citizen advocates.

When I am confident . . .

I Do	I Don't	I Feel
have a positive attitude	feel sorry for myself	OK
behave assertively	grumble	more lively
take on a challenge	blame others	positive
walk tall	slouch	energetic
achieve things	laze about	alert
relax	eat so much	happy

But do you have to wait until you feel confident before you do the things suggested in the first I Do column? What if you tried to do these things anyway? Could there be a beneficial impact on your confidence and capability if you try to adopt a positive attitude, behave assertively, take on challenges, walk tall, achieve things and relax? Remember that you will be working from a position of strength by seeking opportunities to use your skills, assets and talents.

Action Points

- **Who's on your team?** - Make a note of the people who give you the following kinds of support:

- Someone who cares for you unconditionally.

- Someone who always makes you feel good about yourself.

- Someone on whom you can depend in a crisis.

- Someone who listens to you.

- Someone who challenges you.

- Someone who helps you relax.

- Someone who looks to you for advice.

- Someone who encourages you to fly to new heights.

  What do your answers tell you about the extent of your support? Have you a broad spread of friends, family and colleagues? Or is it confined to one or two people? Could you widen it, fill any gaps, make any changes?

- **Holding on and letting go** - What are you still holding on to that holds you back? Do you carry old hurts, prejudices, grievances, wounded pride, illusions of superiority / inferiority, old messages, attitudes and behaviours that limit you? Let go. Have a spring clean. Be forgiving of yourself and toward others. Open a few windows and let some air in!

- **Symbols of support** - Think of a particular occasion in your life when you felt happy and at peace with the world. Recapture that feeling now by visualising the occasion in as much detail as possible. Find a particular word, a gesture, an image or a small object which symbolises that experience and which you can then use to trigger these pleasant feelings to support yourself any time you need it. I can often invoke a feeling of well-being by visualising a perfect summer's day in a country garden. Visualisation is a very powerful technique, both for relaxation and in positive thinking generally.

- **Positive potential** - Make a note here of some of the most important things you know and have learned which will remind you of your positive potential:

Now I know _____
Now I have _____
Now I feel _____
Now I want _____
Now I can _____
Now I will _____

- **Keep a 'fuzzy file'** - Keep a file of cherished letters, cards, photos, references, certificates, newspaper cuttings, favourite sayings and poems etc to record your achievements, boost your confidence and promote warm 'fuzzy' feelings on darker days.

- **Pause for thought** - One of my clients, having worked her way through the book, likened her thinking to choosing and shaping pieces of patchwork to make up a quilt. She now has many of the pieces she wants, of different colours and patterns, but they remain to be added to, combined and sewn to make the finished article. And the variations are enormous . . .

Summing Up . . .

Caring for yourself is not an option, it is a necessity. Taking care of your own needs - physical, emotional and spiritual - is your personal responsibility. You can't look after other people unless you look after yourself.

Self-care will mean different things to you in different circumstances. When things are going smoothly and you're getting on with life, self-care can be about re-charging the batteries and tuning the engine. But when the going gets tough and all but the toughest have got up and gone, self-care becomes a different concept. At this point, it goes way beyond vitamin supplements and a yoga class.

Whatever form 'the slings and arrows of outrageous fortune' take in your life, it's your inner resources which will protect as well as empower you. Adopting a holistic approach to self-care, by striving for harmony and wholeness, will help you align your actions with your priorities and values. It will also give you the strength and confidence to *do what you can do* and *be what you can be* as you claim your own future and make it happen.

Lines from one of Heather Davidson's poems illustrate this perspective:

My journey has just taken a more turbulent course
I use strength, courage and love as the pure driving force.

And Finally . . .

The people whose stories appear in these pages have enriched my life. They personify the idea of self-growth and development, because they have all found ways forward to claim a more positive future. This book is about them, but it's also about you and me.

So consider its relevance to your own experience. Use it as a catalyst - a spur to action. You can dip into it, skip back and forth between chapters, practise the goal-setting method, develop certain Action Points perhaps, and follow up your particular interests through the further reading and addresses sections of the Help List. Working in a group can offer substantial support and encouragement, so if this interests you, find out what courses and other opportunities are available by contacting your local library, college and community projects.

You have one life and endless choices. You may be a keen, reluctant or desperate traveller, but whatever path you choose to take and however long or rough the road, celebrate your own journey. And don't forget to pause along the way to enjoy the view.

In the words of a well-loved Celtic blessing:

May the road rise to meet you and the wind be always at your back.

Help List

- (i) Useful addresses
- (ii) Further reading

(i) Useful addresses

Alcoholics Anonymous
General Office, PO Box 1, Stonebow House, Stonebow,
York YO1 2NJ
Tel: 01904 644026 (see telephone directory for your local
group)

Body & Soul (Mind, Body, Spirit books and tapes)
52 Hamilton Place, Edinburgh EH3 5AX
Tel: 0131 226 3066 (mail order catalogue available)

British Agencies for Adoption and Fostering
Tel: 0171 593 2000

British Association for Counselling
Information Service
Tel: 01788 578328

CRUSE Bereavement Care
Tel: 0181 332 7227 (for further information about services
/ telephone counselling)

Depression Alliance
Tel: 0171 633 9929

Equal Opportunities Commission
Overseas House, Quay Street, Manchester M3 3HN
Tel: 0161 833 9244

Institute for Complementary Medicine
PO Box 194, London SE16 1QZ
(for register of therapists in UK)

MIND (National Association for Mental Health)
Mail Order Service, 15 -19 Broadway, London E15 4BQ
Tel: 0181 519 2122

Personal growth and other workshops
Findhorn Foundation, The Park, Forres, Moray IV36 3TZ
Tel: 01309 690311

Headway National Head Injuries Association
Tel: 0115 924 0800

Health Education Board for Scotland
Library and Information Services, The Priory, Canaan Lane,
Edinburgh EH10 4SG
Tel: 0645 125 442

There is no parallel organisation to HEBS in England. There
is however a network of health promotion units throughout
the country - see local telephone directory for details.

National Council for Voluntary Organisations
Regent's Wharf, 8 All Saints Street, London N1 9RL
Tel: 0171 713 6161

Training, Employment, Careers Guidance
Learning Direct: free information about learning and careers
Tel: 0800 100 900

Your local library is a good point of contact. Also: Training
Access Points, Job Centres, Community Education and
Careers Advisory services, Colleges of Further and Higher
Education.

Open University
Walton Hall, Milton Keynes MK7 6AA
Tel: 01908 653231 (course information line)

HELP LIST

National Drugs Helpline
Tel: 0800 666600 (free, 24-hour confidential counselling, advice and information - calls will not appear on itemised 'phone bills)

Release
(National agency specialising in legal issues surrounding drugs)
Tel: 0171 729 9904 (drugs advice line - office hours)
Tel: 0171 603 8654 - emergency telephone service outside office hours

Samaritans (see local telephone directory)
National helpline: 0345 909090

Skill: National Bureau for Students with Disabilities
336 Brixton Road, London SW9 7AA
Tel / minicom: 0171 274 0565

Skill (Scotland)
Norton Park, 57 Albion Road, Edinburgh EH7 5QY
Tel: 0131 475 2348

Women's Aid Federation of England
(National charity for women and children experiencing physical, sexual or emotional abuse in their homes)
Tel: 0117 944 4411
Helpline: 0345 023 468

Scottish Women's Aid
Tel: 0131 475 2372

Welsh Women's Aid
Tel: 01222 390874

Northern Ireland Women's Aid
Tel: 01232 249041

(ii) Further reading

The Penguin Careers Guide
Anna Alson and Anne Daniel (1996)

The Diving Bell And The Butterfly
Jean-Dominique Bauby (Fourth Estate 1997)

Simple Abundance - A Daybook Of Comfort And Joy
Sarah Ban Breathnach (Bantam 1998)

A Woman In Your Own Right
Anne Dickson (Quartet 1992)

The Handbook Of Alternative And Complementary Medicine - The Essential Health Companion
S Fulder (Vermilion 1997)

Emotional Intelligence
Daniel Goleman (Bantam 1996)

Inside Organisations
Charles Handy (BBC Books 1996)

Staying OK
Thomas Harris with Amy Bjork Harris (Arrow 1995)

Transitions - The Challenge Of Change
Hopson, Scally & Stafford (Management Books 2000, 1993)

Feel The Fear And Do It Anyway
Susan Jeffers (Arrow 1991)

Assert Yourself
Gael Lindenfield (Thorsons, 1986)

The Relate Guide To Better Relationships
Sarah Litvinoff (Vermilion 1998)

Zen And The Art Of Motorcycle Maintenance
Robert M Pirsig (Vintage 1989)

Dorothy Rowe's Guide To Life
(HarperCollins 1995)

Stress: An Owner's Manual
Arthur Rowshan (Oneworld 1997)

The Road Less Travelled
M Scott Peck (Arrow 1990)

Women Returners Guide
Linda Stoker (Bloomsbury 1991)

You Just Don't Understand - Women And Men In Conversation
Deborah Tannen (Virago 1996)

Instant Calm
Paul Wilson (Penguin 1995)

Meditations For Women Who Do Too Much
Anne Wilson Schaef (HarperCollins 1990)

Meditations For Men Who Do Too Much
Jonathon Lazear (HarperCollins 1993)

Springboard - Women's Development Workbook
Liz Willis and Jenny Daisley (Hawthorn Press 1990)

The Huge Bag Of Worries
This booklet is aimed primarily at schoolchildren, and is written by Virginia Ironsides. Single copies are available free of charge from Children 1st, 41 Polwarth Terrace, Edinburgh EH11 1NU. Please send a large SAE.

Further Titles

Help Yourself To A Job

Jackie Lewis ISBN 1-86144-033-2
£7.99 147 pp

Jackie Lewis's practical guide will give you the 'think smart' job-hunting skills you need to compete in today's tough market. She tackles head-on the special problems encountered by career-changers, or those already unemployed. Her simple activities will boost your confidence and get you thinking and moving towards your job goal right away. Jackie has helped hundreds of Job Club clients find the job they wanted using this creative person-centred approach.

Forget The Fear Of Food

Dr Christine Fenn ISBN 1-86144-035-9
£7.99 148 pp

Stop dieting and start living! A leading nutritionist explains why slimming diets don't work, and shows how developing self-esteem is the key to changing our eating habits. Packed with practical tips and activities to help you gain control over your eating and your life.

'A new approach . . . grab this book' *Dr Mary Cursiter*

Subfertility: A Caring Guide For Couples

Dr Phyllis Mortimer ISBN 1-86144-025-1
£7.99 104pp

Dr Mortimer gives a thorough and easy to understand
explanation of the why, when and hows of conception,
arming couples with the information they need to start
looking at possible causes and solutions. She provides
expert advice, encouragement and practical help to
couples experiencing both major and minor fertility
problems.

A Parent's Guide To Drugs

Judy Mackie ISBN 1-86144-028-6
£7.99 103 pp

Judy Mackie's no-nonsense guide addresses the
questions about drugs that concern parents most, and
arms them with the information they need to
communicate effectively with their children. Whether
you suspect your child, or their friends, may be taking
drugs, or are simply worried by the horror stories and
headlines - this practical guide will take you through
the facts and basic steps, which you can use and
develop to suit your own circumstances.

Education Matters

David Abbott ISBN 1-86144-029-4
£7.99 123 pp

Help yourself to some parent power and help your child get the most out of education. If you've ever felt confused by the new curriculum, or by school administration, don't be. Teacher David Abbott cuts through the jargon with straight facts and clear advice. Covers all you need to know, from what the Education Act means for your child, to how to check your child's real progress and talk to their teacher. Any parent can use this practical guide to help their child become a winner.

A Parent's Guide To Dyslexia And Other Learning Difficulties

Maria Chivers ISBN 1-86144-026-X
£7.99 123 pp

Many learning difficulties, once identified, can be overcome. If your child has, or you suspect they might have, learning difficulties, this essential guide gives you the facts you need to take action. It takes you step by step through diagnosis, treatment, education, and beyond into career options. Up-to-the minute facts and practical advice from the founder of the Swindon Dyslexia Centre, herself the mother of dyslexic sons.

Starting School

Lyn Carter ISBN 1-86144-031-6
£7.99 123 pp

Gives the information and advice you need to help
your child to a happy and positive primary school
experience. Shows how to plan for a good start, and
suggests how to deal with problems that might come
up. A good start to primary school lays the foundation
for a successful education for your child. This book
will help you create an enjoyable experience your child
can build on in the future.

The Facts About The Menopause

Elliot Philipp ISBN 1-86144-034-0
£7.99 150 pp Pub Feb 98

Elliot Philipp, a consultant gynaecologist, answers the
questions women most often ask about the
menopause, its symptoms and treatments. He explains
what the menopause is, evaluates HRT and alternative
therapies, and offers practical advice on problems
which can occur at this time.

This complete guide gives women the facts they need
to approach their menopausal years with confidence.

Make The Most Of Your Retirement

Mike Mogano ISBN 1-86144-037-5
£7.99 150 pp Pub Feb 98

Why shouldn't you expect your retirement to be fun?
asks Mike Mogano. Your retirement can be an
expanding world of opportunity, if you organise your
finances first, and look out for problems that can come
up. Plus he offers hundreds of ideas for ways to use
your new-found freedom. Thoughtful discussion and
creative suggestions help you make the most of the life
you've been waiting for.

Thank you for buying a book from Need2Know.
We hope you found it an enjoyable read and a useful
guide. Need2Know produce a wide range of
informative guides for people in difficult situations.
Available in all good bookshops, or alternatively direct
from:

Need2Know, 1-2 Wainman Road, Woodston,
Peterborough PE2 7BU

Order Hotline: 01733 390801   Fax: 01733 230751

Titles

____ Buying A House £5.99
____ Stretch Your Money £4.99
____ Breaking Up £5.99
____ Superwoman £4.99
____ Work For Yourself And Win £5.99
____ The Expatriate Experience £6.99
____ You And Your Tenancy £5.99
____ Improving Your Lifestyle £5.99
____ Safe As Houses £5.99
____ The World's Your Oyster £5.99
____ Everything You Need2Know About Sex £5.99
____ Travel Without Tears £5.99
____ Prime Time Mothers £5.99
____ Parenting Teenagers £5.99
____ Planning Your Wedding £5.99